G000167679

BERNARD V

BEDFORDHIKE

A selection of his Sketch-books from

the Bedfordshire Magazine 1947–98

Edited by Gordon Vowles

The
Book
Castle

First published November 2007
by
The Book Castle
12 Church Street
Dunstable
Bedfordshire
LU5 4RU
www.book-castle.co.uk

in conjunction with
Willington Local History Group
& Bedfordshire Historical Record Society

ISBN 978-1-903747-88-9

Typeset and designed by Caroline and Roger Hillier
The Old Chapel Graphic Design
www.theoldchapellivinghoe.com

Printed in Great Britain
by TJ International Ltd, Padstow, Cornwall

Front and back cover: Church of St. George and Manor Farm, Edworth
Title page: Church of St. Lawrence, Willington

Contents

Editor's Foreword 4

Preface: Biographical Sketch of Bernard West
by Robin Chrystal 7

Selection of Sketch-books in alphabetical order
by location of town or parish 11

Editor's Foreword

For fifty years, from the Summer of 1947 until the Spring of 1998, Bernard West contributed his Sketch-book of drawings and comment to the quarterly issues of the now sadly defunct *Bedfordshire Magazine*, which provided a miscellany and review of Bedfordshire life and history. During that time on two occasions only – in the Autumn of 1958 and the Autumn of 1972 – did he not produce a sketch for publication. This was a remarkable feat, making him by far the longest and most prolific contributor to the Magazine. It was an achievement which not only demonstrates Bernard's commitment to the Magazine but also his extensive knowledge of and intense feeling for his native County.

Bernard was a man of many accomplishments: in his professional life he was a successful practising architect and his 'spare time' interests included history, archaeology, natural history of all sorts and the conservation both of the natural and the best of the man-made environment. These sketches display, in particular, his abilities as an artist of buildings and the landscape, although he was also a specialist in wildlife and botanical illustration. As much as he loved it, the sketches are seldom of the countryside alone. They are more frequently of village and townscape scenes. In some instances, a distinctive building is the sole subject of the drawing. Only in the case of church interiors (where the draughtsmanship of the architect is most apparent) are the sketches devoid of natural forms, usually magnificent and carefully observed trees. Only in some sketches do sylph-like figures, so beloved of architects in their drawings, strike a relatively unreal note. Public houses are frequently referred to in the written commentaries. It is fairly certain that he would have crossed their portals and taken liquid refreshment once his sketches were complete!

An important complement to the drawings of the Sketch-book are the accompanying written commentaries. It was in these writings that he shared with others his detailed knowledge of architecture and the history of Bedfordshire. It was there, too, in a trenchant and often scathing manner that he waged his unrelenting campaign for good design and sympathetic preservation.

In the mid-1950s he contributed, together with his brother-in-law, Sandy Chrystal, a series of nine articles in the *Bedfordshire Magazine* under the general title 'Prospect and Retrospect', in which, taking the County area by area, they examined the physical effects on the environment of a changing social order. In the days before the operation of tight planning controls, they expressed concern at the way villages and towns had been allowed to proliferate so untidily, resulting in places losing their individuality, and anonymity spreading everywhere. They railed, in particular, against the desolate no-man's-land between Luton and Dunstable.

In his Sketch-book commentaries he was a persistent and caustic critic of those who, in his own words, were 'guilty of inducing in others an anaesthetic acceptance of ugliness'. Constantly in the commentaries, he remonstrated against blight and eyesores in the environment, ribbon development and scruffy urban sprawl, housing estates which were contrived rather than designed, town decay, derelict buildings, litter problems, garish and ill-placed advertisements, poor street furniture and, most frequently, the insensitive siting of poles, pylons and overhead wires, especially, in the case of the latter, when they cluttered the subjects he wished to draw. Such was his invective that occasionally he was accused of bigotry and prejudice. Certainly, he favoured conservation rather than restoration and, at times, he was perhaps harsher than many might now feel appropriate on the restoration work of some Victorian architects. Be that as it may, it is also true that his comments were always perceptive and lively, and certainly never dull. In expressing his great love and concern for both the natural and the man-made environment, what he was endeavouring to promote was – again, in his own words – 'the creation of structures which grow out of the landscape and follow its harmonies'.

For over forty years Bernard lived in Willington at Home Close, an extended thatched cottage, and when a few years ago it was decided to try and form a local history group in the village, he gave the idea his enthusiastic support. He attended the inaugural meeting but was sadly not well enough to take any further part before his death in January 2006. Some members of the Group felt that something should be done to mark Bernard's unique contribution to the record of Bedfordshire life in the 20th century. And so the idea emerged of a commemorative volume of a selection of his Sketch-book drawings and writings which appeared over the years in the *Bedfordshire Magazine*. To bring the idea to fruition has required the support and help of a number of people.

As editor of the volume, and on behalf of the Willington Local History Group, I should like to thank the following: the Trustees of the Estate of Bernard West for agreeing to the reproduction of all the original material; the Chairman and Council Members of the Bedfordshire Historical Record Society as owners of the copyright of the publications of the White Crescent

Press and White Rock; Ann Collett-White, last Editor of the *Bedfordshire Magazine*, for the loan of the Editor's set of volumes of the magazine; Robin Chrystal for contributing the biographical sketch of his uncle; Richard West for his enthusiastic encouragement throughout and for making available the original of the photograph of his father taken by Keith Lazenby and used on page 11; and, above all, Paul Bowes of the Book Castle for his backing of the publication.

In selecting the Sketch-book entries for inclusion in the volume, I have endeavoured to give a representative spread throughout the whole County although Bernard, in fact, chose to draw more locations in the north and middle of the County than in the south – in a busy life he inevitably chose those nearer home. I have omitted a number of sketches where he returned to the same site more than once; over the years he sketched the 'beauty spots' of Felmersham, Odell, Sutton and Woburn on no less than four occasions each. There were also other entries where the written text seemed unduly dated or contained obscure references. The aim has been to include entries which combine a distinctive drawing and informative and entertaining writing.

It is to be hoped that this selection of Bernard's Sketch-books will not only serve as a fitting tribute to the man but also bring to the attention of a new and wider audience his talents as artist and commentator. Rather than being just thumbed and read, the volume might also be used in a practical way by encouraging readers to visit the sites he sketched. There, it would be possible to observe what changes have taken place in the intervening years since Bernard made his sketches and determine whether, as he wrote in his commentaries, his worst fears have sadly come to pass or the Bedfordshire countryside and its buildings have, so far, been preserved for our continued enjoyment. As Bernard still reminds us all so forcibly in his writings: the price of survival remains eternal vigilance.

Gordon Vowles
Willington, May 2007

Preface

Artist, naturalist and architect – Bernard West was all of these, but he was also a great character and conversationalist. He liked nothing better than a good natter and my fondest memories of him will always be of lunchtimes in his local pub, the *Crown* at Willington, arguing and discussing over a pint.

Too many people are bland, lack thought through opinions or are reluctant to test their views in debate. Bernard was never guilty of those sins. Two examples from the notes he wrote to accompany his Sketch-books in the *Bedfordshire Magazine* give a flavour of the sort of man he was.

Take this comment about the destruction wrought on Bedford: 'There is so much sad and disastrously wrong with the County town, not least its appalling traffic problems, that it is probably wiser not to make enemies locally but to make a few on a wider front.' Or these lines on Tempsford: 'The limes around God's little acre at Tempsford are not how God intended limes to be, but stunted, crippled and belittled. There should be a high grand canopy as at Cople, but the trees are reduced to the semblance of giant lavatory brushes when seen in winter, which is unforgivable.'

That's vintage Bernard: outspoken, opinionated – not afraid to offend – thought provoking, passionate, advocating change. Life was never a weak watercolour with Bernard.

He was drawing for the *Bedfordshire Times* whilst still a schoolboy. Whilst on National Service he ended up in the Russian sector of Berlin – rather the worse for wear. He worked with the poet laureate Sir John Betjeman and he designed a coffee bar for the actress Diana Dors. Some found him off putting, especially those not used to having to justify their actions. To me he was stimulating and challenging. He always respected those with whom he disagreed but who were able to argue their case.

Bernard Billing West was born on February 22nd 1926 at 32, Gwyn Street, Bedford. It's long since been swept away and replaced by the town's bus station, now itself about to be replaced by a mixed housing and retail development. (Bernard would have had a view on that.)

He was a pupil at Bedford Modern School where his interest in drawing was encouraged, and thanks to his father, Kenneth, that other lifelong interest, wildlife, was also nurtured. Weekends in the 1930s and 40s would frequently involve cycling all over the Bedfordshire countryside, seeing and hearing things that have long since disappeared not just from the County but now from England as a whole. Take birdlife. Imagine hearing a corncrake by the Ouse at Pavenham or seeing a wryneck in Clapham today! Sightings of either would set twitchers' phone lines humming. Yet Bernard remembered seeing both in his youth.

After school Bernard went to University College, London, to study architecture but, in common with so many others, National Service intervened. He later called those years some of the best of his life and it's easy to see why. While some might have spent their time square-bashing or been stationed in some God-forsaken spot, Bernard landed on his feet. He was involved in setting up the first children's school for servicemen's families in West Germany and next joined a team helping illiterate army personnel. It was then that he met Leonard Rossiter, later to find fame as Rigsby in television's *Rising Damp*, and the two certainly hit it off. Secondment to the Czech Army followed during that all too brief period before Czechoslovakia fell under Stalin's control. There were official banquets, visits to provincial towns and the joys of Prague after the devastation of war-torn Germany. Not bad for a young man who before that had known little other than Bedfordshire.

Back in London he graduated and took up architecture and for a while was on the edge of a group that included the Chelsea Arts Club for which he painted sets for their annual balls.

A major turning point came when Bernard returned to Bedford and set up a small architect's practice with my father, Sandy Chrystal. They were to work together for the next thirty years. It was quite a partnership: the one practical, good at business and figures, the other colourful and erratic and with a penchant for unusual antics. One hot summer afternoon I remember wandering into the office of Chrystal & West to find Bernard stretched out on the floor, sound asleep. Together they built up a reputation for restoration projects and went on to win several hotly contested awards, including a national Heritage Award in 1975 from the Civic Trust for the restoration of Basmead Manor, and in 1980 the Good Design in Housing Award for Bunyan's Mead in Elstow.

Bernard always said that my father kept him sane as he grappled down the years with his most hated species, council planners, whom he always saw as intent on wantonly curbing his artistic creations. There were victories over the planners but also defeats. One of the most galling concerned not a single building but a whole townscape – and a key one at that. In 1969 a Chrystal and West scheme called for the traffic to be taken out of St. Paul's Square in the centre of Bedford and for the Castle Lane area to be redeveloped. It was asking the planners to cast aside their love affair with the car and in the 1960s that was anathema. It got precisely nowhere. Now, nearly forty years on, some elements of that forward thinking plan might finally be about to occur.

But if planners were a challenge for Bernard, winning over his future wife's father proved to be one too. Bernard met Judith during an archaeological dig at Old Warden. Bernard and my father were burrowing away and my mother, Jill, introduced the couple. They later said they met 'over touching spades'. That was the easy part. Judith's father was Kenneth Western. At his height he was one of the most famous music hall and radio stars in the land – one half of the Western Brothers. With marriage in the air he sent this note to the man known in the family as 'Sandy's funny friend'.

"As part of the premium for the fairly delicate hand of the daughter Judith, you will please let me have the following information by return of post: the names of at least a dozen well known moths of this county and where and when they can be found, such things as markings and subsoil and their rarity.
The names of societies to which you moth men belong – a few Latin names would be appreciated.
You are welcome to join me at my table ... You are asked *not* to bring sandwiches.
Signed by the Governor, typed by Tadpole, who is the overall boss in this house, Judith's beloved mother and famous ash dropper."

Quite a reception committee!

But Bernard won through and his future mother-in-law later became Chrystal & West's secretary, a job she continued with until well into her seventies.

Architecture, drawing and painting, a family, more than enough you might think for a full life, but Bernard's childhood interest in wildlife (or what was then more commonly known as natural history), also flourished. In the 1950s and 60s naturalists were seen as fuddy-duddies and all but guaranteed to be the butt of humour. The concept of conservation was new and alien to many.

But along with others Bernard was one of the founder members of the Bedfordshire and Huntingdonshire Wildlife Trust back in 1959. There were eighty-five members then but their goal was an ambitious one – to safeguard wild places for future generations to enjoy. Now the Trust manages more than 5000 acres of woodland, hillside, marsh and meadow – a living legacy to Bernard and those other early pioneers.

It was at one of those reserves at Felmersham that as a teenager I got to know Bernard. He would pick me up on winter Sunday mornings, and with Radio Three as backdrop, we would head off for a session of fencing, digging or damming. As a fourteen and fifteen year old what I found most refreshing was that Bernard treated me as an adult, an equal, listened to my opinions and respected them. He treated everyone this way and there was never any side to him. Although he was very knowledgeable about wildlife he deferred to me when it came to birds and it was due to him that I developed what has become a life long interest.

He also introduced me to alcohol. After our stint on the reserve we would repair to the *Bell* at Odell where Bernard would down a frothy pint – or two – of Abbott. It took me some time to join him but he thankfully steered me away from the diluted joys of English lager – or 'gnat's piss' as Bernard called it. In later life I relished my lunchtimes with him at the *Crown* in Willington which was his second living room. So many stimulating debates: the hypocrisy of the British attitude to sex; the role of the Royal family; our common European past; religion's role in our irreligious society; deference; the efficacy of species reintroduction in the wild; did good music end with Elgar? Tankard in hand Bernard would argue his case, with knowledge and humour and always with a good grace.

Robin Chrystal, 2007

A SELECTION OF
BERNARD WEST'S SKETCH-BOOKS

from the Bedfordshire Magazine

1947–98

AMPTHILL

For many years a blot on the otherwise reasonably fair face of central Ampthill, No. 110 Dunstable Street, sometime Home Guard and Liberal Party headquarters, was fast becoming a ruin, with all the ills to which an old building is subject in destructive control. An enlightened property company bought the building and inaugurated a scheme of restoration, and in a reasonable number of years will see a return from rentals to compensate for its initial outlay.

It was decided to regularize the façade again and obliterate the dreadful Victorian shop-front on the Woburn Street – Dunstable Street corner, to replace the glazing-bars in the first-floor windows and to re-use the old doorcase in the form of a free-standing porch. This last feature provides a sheltered entrance to the three shops on the ground floor. Much of the roof and other parts of the structure had to be replaced because of extensive damage by dry rot, and it is probably true to say that the building is now sounder than when it was first erected.

My illustration shows two of the controversial street lights; but there are more offensive pieces of street furniture in the centre of the town than these. One, for example, is the hideous lamp-cum-signpost on the Woburn Street corner, and Sir William Chamber's pump would look happier if its base were not engulfed in earth – why not use the more suitable urban grouping of a few tubs of flowers?

The newsagent's premises, a spiky essay in Victorian Jacobean by Blore, serves as a rather restless plinth for the old market clock, which must have looked more at ease on the old market house than it does now. This little cupola of the late 17th century is a simple example of a favourite skyline feature of that period which reached its greatest refinement at Coleshill, now tragically burnt and gone.

Winter 1962

AMPTHILL – Church Street

The illustration shows a present-day view of that part of Ampthill which has survived the most perfectly. The imposing block on the left is Avenue House, built between 1790–1800 and a perfect grouping of its period. The carving of the stone frieze on the porch is especially lovely.

Up the hill the view is terminated by those houses which grouped around the church give something of the effect of a miniature cathedral close, their quiet red brick dignity contrasting with the brown sandstone of the church and the white gothic of its church built windows.

High on the right the central detail of Foulislea House can just be seen and then in steep perspective some of the delightful bow windowed fronts running down to the Ampthill News Office, itself a Georgian design of outstanding merit, preserved by discrimination and feeling which is only too rare nowadays. Ampthill is in fact fortunate that so much has survived within its boundaries, and although the entry into the town from Bedford has been marred in recent years when the necessary widening could so easily have added dignity, there is hope when one sees the good intentions of the bank block by the White Hart, which in its unashamedly traditional design blends quite well into the scene. We trust that the iconoclasts' recent proposal to thrust away the old Town Pump from its traditional Market Place site to some obscure position will not be permitted. Ampthill's individuality needs careful watching and protection.

Autumn 1949

AMPTHILL – John Cross Hospital

Hidden behind Coopers Hill and properly visible only from Station Road, this pleasing late 17th-century building is missed by many visitors. It has an important place in Ampthill's architectural development, for it represents the start of a tradition that culminated in the urbane refinement of Foulislea and Avenue House, although later rebuilding has effaced it in the body of the town.

John Cross founded his Oxford hospital as almshouses for eight men and four women, with a matron and a reader, and his architect made a sound job of satisfying this schedule of accommodation, incorporating a chapel into the bargain and siting the whole with a good southern aspect. Its major interest lies in the excellence of its details, which are quite sophisticated for its period, particularly the fine wooden cornice, though the style of the mullioned and transomed windows survives from an earler tradition.

Coopers Hill in the background, a fine piece of heathland within the urban area, is officially scheduled as a 'site of scientific interest'. Inadvertently reduced by ploughing in recent years, it was one of those unfortunate cases where the owner had not been notified of its status in the County Development Plan, a state of affairs which the newly formed Naturalists' Trust seeks to remedy. Many plants and insects of great rarity and interest are found in this limited area, but luckily in this case the ploughing has not seriously affected the habitats.

Inevitably, perhaps, more of Station Road will be developed, but so long as buildings are erected only on its south side the best interests of Ampthill residents will be served. Northwards towards the Woburn Road the country is too fine to be sacrificed, no matter what the demands may be.

Spring 1962

John Cross, Almshouses, Ampthill, Bedfordshire
January 1962 Gerald B. West.

ARLESEY

South-east Bedforshire is a landscape which could ill afford to be urbanised in the way it has been since the turn of the century. It must once have been the sort of open country which still survives as one approaches Wrestlingworth from the north, the old settlements standing out as tree clumps, a church tower and a huddle of barns and houses. The development associated with the airfield has made a sprawl of Henlow, although surprisingly enough there is some style and maturity around the camp itself, but places like Stotfold, Clifton, Shefford and Arlesey are largely amorphous, dreary and have completely denied us the open view and a chance of enjoying the landscape in any breadth. With a little elevation at Lower Stondon the hills appear and there are occasional views of Henlow and Langford, which from a distance can still evoke the landscape of the mid-19th century, but not until the Great North Road has been crossed is one free of the sprawl, coming to Ashwell in the right way across open fields.

It is too late to plan for compact communities, the chance having been largely lost, so instead one seeks for the soul of a place; that part of the settlement when the pattern is informal and the result of slow growth. It should be around the church at Arlesey but is not: one pub and a handsome though decayed cottage, elegantly combining thatch and tile, are really the only survivors. The rest is housing estate anonymity.

Further south, however, one is suddenly aware of a sense of place: there is for a start a rash of pubs ranging from Greene King under thatch, picturesque externally, sterile inside, to a heavy-handed job in brewers' Tudor, a Whitbread contribution to the scene. There are houses on to the pavement, walls and carefully maintained hedges, and at once the view, made up of elements fairly unimportant in themselves, composes into the picturesque. Whatever one's county loyalty this is not an adjective which can be generally applied to the landscape of east Bedfordshire, and one is, as they say, grateful for small mercies.

Winter 1974

ASPLEY GUISE – Aspley House

This house, built in 1690, has been attributed to Wren. Although I know of no evidence to support this link with the great architect of the English Renaissance, much work of his inspiration was realized in terms of plans and elevations by his assistants. These men gathered around the master throughout his long life, forming something similar to the modern architectural office and at the same time a 'school' with its own very individual vernacular.

The English scene is hard to imagine without such gracious houses of mellow red brick or stone, as in the small towns of Woburn or Ampthill, or set in their few acres as here at Aspley. Since the war Aspley House has returned to the peace of private occupation; it is furnished with taste and a notable collection of Chinese porcelain graces several of the fine rooms. Of architectural significance is the late 18th-century fireplace in the hall, which is a wonderful example of the refinement of the style for which the brothers Adam were mainly responsible. It employs the delightful honeysuckle or anthemion ornament which was introduced during this period. The contemporary fittings of the grate are very fine.

The setting of the house, framed by great cedars and surrounded by a small, well-timbered park, makes one forget for a time the pits of the clay vale just over the brow of the hill.

Summer 1951

ASTWICK – Bury Farm

A moated farmstead with the name of Bury indicates considerable antiquity. At one time it seems likely that the nearby Ivel fed the moat, until the river was dug out in 1847 and straightened in conjunction with the modernisation of the mill. When the moat itself was cleaned out recently a rich deposit of oyster shells was found, giving some idea of the living standards of such a site in the Middle Ages and subsequently; the diet was not all turnips and salted meat. The Great North Road was a supply route not only from London but also Colchester: the noisy eastern boundary of the parish now, it was an artery of trade before the railways, mainly of vegetables for the London markets.

Around the moat and in the gardens of Bury Farm there are numbers of architectural fragments; mostly pier sections, round and keeled, they indicate a date in the mid-1300s, and one supposes originate from the now rather sad and truncated little church of St. Guthlac. There are only two such dedications in England, Guthlac having lived as a hermit in the Lincolnshire Fens. The dedication may originate within the old diocese of Lincoln, in the days when Buckden was the country seat of the Bishop. It is obvious that the church was once larger from the blocked arch in the south side of the tower. This was into a transept presumably, and might well indicate the tower was once central.

Bury Farm is from appearances a 17th-century building, with a dignified late 18th–early 19th-century elevation to the moat, lovely topiaried yews and extensive outbuildings. These, black tarred now, must once have been feather edge boarded with pantiled roofs. A southern range survives in the original form, giving some impression of the former magnificent appearance of these buildings.

The setting of Astwick is lovely after the nearby straggle of Stotfold. Church Farm, St. Guthlac's and its adjoining cottage, with the 18th-century vicarage behind, are so spaced and sited that any infilling of the village should be strongly resisted, particularly in the little paddock which forms a foreground to the church.

Summer 1990

Bury Farm Astwick March '90
Bernard Watt. R.I.B.A.

BARTON

The hill-foot villages of the Chilterns have suffered from the 20th century nearly as much as the towns. There is nothing between the Thames and Hitchin quite so ghastly as the Dunstable/Luton sprawl, and Barton has lost its relationship with the scarp slope of the downs through expansion, but all along the hills to a greater or lesser extent there are the same painful contrasts. The great beech hangers and rolling skyline at Pitstone are reduced to insignificance by the cement works; Wendover and Halton are set in once attractive country where the RAF in flimsy but permanent accommodation seems to have spread as widely as possible; Aston Rowant is ruined by a piece of wilful and barbaric motorway planning. Thus the pearls of the Chiltern scarp are few, such as Ewelme, Watlington, Ellesborough and Cymbeline's Mount – but all too often hill-foot suburbanisation on the Barton pattern blurs the relationship of the Vale of Aylesbury with the hills.

At Barton, the estates spread along the Higham Gobion road have become a textbook example of failure in planning control, but behind them is a precarious survival: the church, a magnificent partly-moated rectory and various 18th-century cottages. Some are in the usual fancy dress, and one in the foreground of the illustration sorely in need of repair, but we must be grateful that it is still possible to walk from here onto downland, and still feel the relationship of the spring-line village with the hills beyond.

Barton church contains remains of the Totternhoe school of 13th-century carving in the form of a lovely respond of clustered columns with a foliated capital, and externally is typically Chiltern, crumbling clunch and flint dressings, now much renewed and in some cases failing badly by being only one cobblestone deep, set in hard cement and spalling off from the soft stone behind. Maintaining such buildings is becoming an increasing burden on dwindling congregations, and one wonders how much longer structures built with such perishable materials can be expected to survive.

Summer 1977

Barton in the Clay April 1977

BARTON HILLS

The chalk hills at Barton mark the limit of the Chiltern range in an easterly direction at the Hitchin gap. Beyond, the lower East Anglian heights undulate from the Gog Magogs through the Breckland to the sea. Barton's intimate and unspoilt slopes display all the characteristics of the chalk hills within a limited area, and the views over what is in fact the Bedfordshire continuation of the Vale of Aylesbury are very fine. In the middle distance lies Wrest Park and eastwards Shillington church stands out on its mound of chalk. To the north the view is terminated by the thick woods of the greensand ridge.

As with all chalk country, these hills are rich with signs of ancient occupation – lynchets, the baulks of Celtic fields and Ravensburgh Castle itself astride the County boundary. Village memory preserves the name of each rounded slope: Bonfire Knoll and the Flagstaff, Primrose and Plum-pudding Hills, the Steps, the Stairway and the rest. On these open hills native orchids succeed the purple pasque flower, and eyebrights and gentians follow the summer vetches and milkworts. Insects and birds are equally varied and interesting.

There is one unhappy note in the lovely valley which winds southwards from Barton church – the piping which hides and confines the springs gushing from the hills. Could not this now be dismantled to allow the springs to flow in the natural and charming way they did years ago?

Autumn 1951

BATTLESDEN

Turning off the Woburn-Hockliffe road into what, without a signpost, might be taken for a farm tract, brings one to as remote and romantic a piece of landscape as any in the County. To the south are the familiar 'blue remembered hills' dominated by Ivinghoe Beacon with a rich foreground, well wooded and undulating and, as in many places in the gault country, strangely reminiscent of distant Wessex.

As a place Battlesden seems hardly to exist and it requires imagination to visualise the original village settlement around the church. Only the Garden House and Battlesden House survive. Battlesden Park is long demolished as part of the Russells' policy of easing out any estate likely to threaten the boundaries of their demesnes. The surviving grounds were of course laid out by Joseph Paxton whose career started as a gardener's boy at the 'big house'. It is an indication of his talents that he rebuilt the house in the 1860s and remodelled the grounds for the son of his original employer.

The church of St. Peter, although heavily repaired, still has that marvellous texture that arises in areas deficient in freestone. Decaying clunch, cobbles, brick, plaster and the precious limestone brought down from the north. The gault brick buttresses with their stone dressings on the south side are for once a fortunate necessity and have weathered beautifully. Of the interior, accessible in spite of the remote situation, it can only be said that it comes near to perfection: simple, whitewashed and tranquil. It contains little of architectural note except the Duncombe monuments of 1603 and later, and there is a clumsy little 12th-century font with wonderfully amateurish leaf carving.

However, there are the brackets either side of the altar, which are really strange. To all intents and purposes they appear to be of late 15th century, with mouldings and other details characteristic of the period. But the supporting angels have the faces of 18th-century cherubs or putti, with a sort of Hogarthian kerchief around their heads. Are they re-cut or 18th century revival Gothick? Their hands in contrast are completely inept in comparison with the well-modelled heads. A small puzzle but one which makes architectural exploration so fascinating.

Winter 1994

BEDFORD – Wing Bridge

By its very function a bridge becomes the focal point of a riverside town, and it should be worthy of its position and its purpose. Bedford is fortunate indeed, for the bridge over the Ouse is an architectural gem judged by any standards; and since its sympathetic widening it also adequately fulfils the needs of modern traffic (although one could have wished, perhaps, for a little architectural dishonesty to hide the surface of the concrete under the new side of the arches).

Francis, Marquis of Tavistock, laid its first stone on April 26th, 1811, and it was opened two years later, on November 1st, in the 52nd year of the reign of George III. The design and execution was by John Wing, a Bedford man. The new bridge replaced an ancient structure which had passed through many vicissitudes, including fearful floods. By 1765 the two guard houses on the bridge were demolished. The chapel had gone at the Reformation, in those far-off days which probably saw Katherine of Aragon cross the river on her unhappy way from Ampthill via Buckden to Kimbolton. The bridges downstream at Huntingdon and St. Ives, the latter still retaining its chapel, show how Bedford's mediaeval bridge must have appeared. For their romantic charm, Wing's bridge has grace and urbanity; it is, in fact, architecture – of the last phase of the classical tradition. The only misfortune is that its neighbour buildings are not at all as well-mannered as the Swan Hotel, particularly on the south bank, but it has a still lovely though depleted frame of trees both upstream and down.

Winter 1950

BEDFORD – St. Cuthbert's Street

Most towns of any antiquity have their quiet backwaters where, away from the roar of through traffic, garish shop-fronts and neon signs, the old street character survives. In these areas of quiet Georgian red brick, stucco and plaster, social levels are mixed as in a village and the differentiations of the suburbs are unknown. They may be only a shadow of what urban life was and still could be, but they have a neighbourliness that the desolate housing estates lack.

St. Cuthbert's, Bedford's only real example, is a precarious survival of such a district, and already one large house has succumbed. Towards St. Peter's the commercial tide is marked, but with a few exceptions is not unreasonable, though there is one jarring juxtaposition of name-boards with a fine Georgian façade. But why should St.Cuthbert's have to suffer one of the most unforgivable pieces of view-wrecking in the town? The wall of advertising in front of the *Ship*, one of the most delightful pubs in Bedford, is an intolerable scandal and deserves the strongest censure.

A street like St. Cuthbert's presents a wonderful opportunity to carry out the sort of urban experiment that is being tried this year by the Civic Trust in Norwich, where the local authority and most of the property owners in Magdalen Street are co-operating in redecorating the whole street to a considered plan. It could be done in Bedford. For a relatively small outlay an already pleasant backwater could become the most delightful street in the town.

Summer 1959

St Cuthberts. April 1959
Bernard B West.

BEDFORD – Mill Street

The Mill Street/St. Cuthbert's junction is a valuable survival of proper urban and urbane values in an area of general exploitation. Newnham Street holds together as far as the *Castle* after which it is disembowelled for the benefit of Gibbs and Dandy, only to come together again after the *Three Cups*. The fate of St. Cuthbert's with the heartless Dormbridge House in the middle is forever sealed, the sensitive detailing of the Merton Centre doing little to save it.

Seen from the first floor window of the offices of Thornton Baker, a perfect example of infill on the old Litson timber yard site, is what the Victorian architects called 'unity by inclusion', something of everything all in one view. In spite of this diversity the grain of the town is preserved, though by no means accidentally: for example, only a public enquiry saved 45–47 Mill Street, now admirably restored.

Wing and Jackson's Bunyan Meeting of 1849, a gawky essay in a sort of sub-Roman Doric, has at present a slightly over-smartened air, not mitigated by the mean wall and gates which were an unfortunate concomitant of chopping a room off the adjoining Howard's House a few years ago. This did great harm to the garden also but gave a smooth run for the motorist to get to the next bottleneck more quickly. We didn't think of traffic-free zones in those days.

Opposite is a perfect Georgian town house, of which we have too few examples: as a neighbour it is elbowed by the hearty bad manners of the old fire station. The days when so small an establishment was adequate to cope with emergencies seem distant indeed, but it is saved for us to enjoy as a lovely piece of assured vulgarity. To leave St. Cuthbert's church to the last, beleaguered on its island, is not to ignore its value. As architecture, particularly internally, one needs a taste for central European 'rundbogenstil', but it can just pass muster as Norman from outside, particularly the tower which is very satisfactory.

Spring 1978

BIGGLESWADE

Biggleswade is dismissed in Pevsner's *The Buildings of England* as having a 'disappointing centre in a visually disappointing little town'. A harsh but undeniably valid judgement and yet the space is generous, with the island of Market Hall and shops in just the right place to prevent the square becoming amorphous.

It is in detail, not the general massing, that the actual disappointment arises. If only there had been one or two good 18th-century town houses or a mediaeval survival here and there; but of course they might have suffered as with so many small towns from the barbaric insertion of shop fronts. Better not to have the architecture perhaps than to have it mutilated.

All the same there are good things. Wing's town hall of 1844 with its great Roman Doric columns and tent-like roof deserves better treatment than it has received. On either side of the five bay centre, symmetry has been lost and the colour is dreadful. This could easily be improved. The *White Hart* is jolly with a proper country town character, though the half timbering is a little dubious. One is at least thankful that the brewery have retained the excellent early 19th-century glazing and not tried to Tudorise the fenestration.

The strange building is the engineering works of Delaney Gallay; one's initial reaction is to dismiss it as out of scale, typical 1930s industrial building in the wrong place, but given some classical detail to make it acceptable. Yet it is rather grand, the shallow projection of the three bay centre is further enriched by the entrance door which is right in scale and detail. A proper pediment to the centre, not the present rather tottering apology, would work wonders and again the colour does nothing for the building.

One often wonders about the island, dedicated inevitably to car parking and bus stops. Given that Biggleswade is the centre of great agricultural prosperity, it could surely afford some semi-mature trees. This would make such a difference and why not fully pedestrianise the east end of the square by the town hall with one or two trees there? It is probably the one town in Bedfordshire which could most benefit from the sort of overall Civic Trust scheme that has transformed other places, many of even less potential. Pevsner's strictures are unconstructive if they mean Biggleswade is inevitably condemned to a future of mediocrity.

Autumn 1986

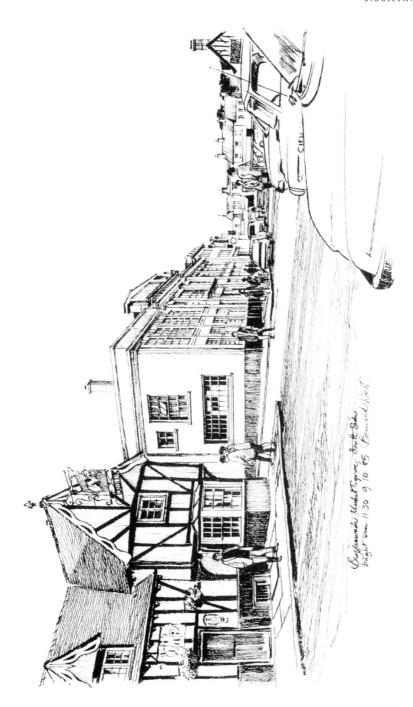

BIGGLESWADE – Wesleyan Chapel

Whether Wesley ever preached in Biggleswade or not, he probably passed through the town several times on his way to Hinxworth and Wrestlingworth. He died in 1791: by 1794 work had begun on the creation of the first society in Biggleswade and had progressed so well that by the early 19th century the old chapel in Cowfairlands had become inadequate for the congregation's needs, so they sold it for £500 and bought a new site from John Elston, a bricklayer, for £620. The new chapel, begun in 1834, was opened in November 1835. The forebuilding or porch, an addition of 1889, is unexpectedly as sensitively detailed as the original structure, with the capitals in the Greek taste that accorded well with 1834, though certainly not with 1889 when a solid Roman style was back in fashion. One must assume that it is by an unusually sympathetic hand, or that old materials have been re-used and set forward.

There are other buildings in the town, less well endowed architecturally but nevertheless good sound work, which could benefit from the lesson in good taste presented by the chapel. Now that the Great North Road, with its dust and noise, has been diverted, Biggleswade should realise that, even if parts of the town are ungracious, it has many buildings which simple repainting would considerably improve. Rumour has it that a 'face-lift' is planned. I hope it will start in the market place, where some of the existing colours are barbarous.

Spring 1963

Biggleswade 1963. Bernard Brett.

BILLINGTON

South of Leighton Buzzard the countryside is rich in a different way from that to the north. It also differs from the remainder of the Vale of Aylesbury, of which it forms a part, in being broken up by a range of low hills, on the end of which stands Billington. Indicated on geological maps as a chalk outlier, the hill shows little evidence of its composition on the site: more likely it belongs to the same range as those at Toddington and is only by chance capped by uneroded chalk because of its proximity to the Totternhoe promentary.

The hilltop is well timbered, and although the village has lost much of its early character the cottage in the illustration is particularly charming. The church, with a rather outlandish Victorian bellcote, is a heavily restored 13th-century building, a typical 'hamlet' church of a small community that has never fluctuated much in population. Like most place-names Billington has undergone some amusing changes before assuming the present form, for instance, Billydon, Bylendon and Billesdon.

The country south of the village is a gentle prelude to the dramatic bulk of the Chiltern scarp, which directly south of the village rises to the well known landmark of Ivinghoe Beacon. At the foot of Billington Hill are broad meadows, heavily timbered hedges and watercourses fringed with willows, which give a strong reminder of the lowlands of distant Somerset; but nearer the chalk hills the landscape becomes more open and around Edlesborough even a little bleak. In the water meadows is to be found one of the botanical treasures of Bedfordshire, the snake's-head fritillary (*Fritillaria meleagris*). It belongs to the lush meadows of the upper Thames, is found in Oxford where it is famed in the Magdalen meadows and occurs sparingly through the Aylesbury vale to Bedfordshire.

Spring 1956

Billington Hill February 1956
Bernard B. West.

BLETSOE – Castle

The St. Johns of Bletsoe of long association with the castle and manor are
eclipsed in many people's minds by the birth here of the Lady Margaret,
mother of Henry VII. John Beauchamp was under age at his father's death in
1420 when the manor passed to his sister and heir, Margaret, then only 11.
Her first husband was Sir Oliver St. John, but it was the child of her second
marriage to John Beaufort, Duke of Somerset, Lady Margaret Beaufort, who
was mother of King Henry. Margaret's life, or what we know of it, invites
speculation; the annulled marriage in childhood to John, Duke of Suffolk,
suggests family manoeuvring. Edmund Tudor was the first official wedlock,
then followed Henry Stafford and finally Thomas Stanley, Earl of Derby. The
consequences of the first adult marriage give Bletsoe a firm place in English
history, one of which Elizabeth I was herself aware as she is reputed to have
made the castle a stop on one of her tours of the Kingdom.

The castle is more accurately a fragment of a vast courtyard house which
on surviving evidence seems to have been started in the late-16th century.
Only the bridge over the moat gives a glimpse of mediaeval work and a lot
here has disappeared since the days when Fisher drew it. The real loss however
since then has been the magnificent third floor with its four Jacobean gables
crowned with balls and pinnacles. This would have been a fine sight had it
survived, backed as we know it was with a range of giant Northamptonshire
style chimney stacks in stone.

What is left, nevertheless, a fine house of unusually pure ashlar work and
the setting in a miniature park of really magnificent trees, is one of the finest
things in North Bedfordshire.

Summer 1968

Bletsoe Castle April 1908.
Bernard B West.

BLUNHAM

Blunham village is one of those 'on the road to nowhere'. In the centre of a triangle of busy roads it has a peace denied to some of its neighbours, and a rather abstracted and sleepy air.

In the church of St. Edmund it possesses one of the finer architectural monuments of the County. The fabric is of mixed local sandstone and limestone, the two stones used alternately in the tower arch as brown and grey stone. The church tower is particularly fine and far older than it looks being basically 12th century – a west door and tower arch internally are the proof. The silhouette of the tower today dates from 1583, a late use of gothic forms.

The interior of the church is magnificent and rich in furnishings, in particular a fine 16th-century stone screen separating the chancel from the south chapel. There is also a lovely tomb recess in the chancel north wall, looking more like an Easter sepulchre, with the same lush 14th century as the Ely Lady Chapel. Also the monument to Susan, Countess of Kent, in alabaster is very fine and dignified.

The church is forever associated with John Donne, but he was an absentee incumbent who out of a probably bad conscience donated a chalice in 1626.

The village centre preserves a core of old buildings picturesquely disposed along wide streets. My view shows a cottage group of the late 17th and early 18th centuries on the north side of the church. As in the cottages on the left, the earlier buildings generally abut gable end on to the street. After the end of the 17th century they are usually aligned parallel to the street as on the right.

Autumn 1952

BOLNHURST – The Old Plough

Northwards from Bedford runs a road which, after it has left the suburban fringes, enters a stretch of country charming in its pastoral of patterned fields, old farms and quiet villages. On its way to dignified Kimbolton it passes through the village of Bolnhurst. Its church stands alone in the fields, some distance from the village, like a number of other churches in Bedfordshire which are detached from the community of which they should form a part – Chellington and Carlton, for example.

The house I illustrate is a typical example of the older type of house in North Bedfordshire – lath and plaster over timber, with gleaming colour-wash that seems to trap and reflect the sunlight, a vivid foil to the green of the trees. This old place, as its name suggests, was once the *Plough Inn*, but an alien, brick-built with pebble dash and roofed with Welsh slates, further up the road, has taken its name away.

Autumn 1947

BROMHAM
– Summer Pastoral, Bromham Park

In spite of much modern building the village still preserves a rural atmosphere, and fortunately most of the modern cottages around the green are of excellent design.

The park, a magnificent stretch of country, is approached from the road through two gateways, each with a charming cottage lodge in the Victorian 'romantic' style. It contains fine beeches near the hall, and ashes, as in my sketch, but the elms have become the prey of the dreaded elm disease.

Picturesquely embowered in trees by the river is the famous hall, an ancient building, quaint and rambling, with memories of the Dyves and Wydviles, and in more recent times of the formidable Miss Rice Trevor, terror of the youthful C. F. Farrar in his early boating days on 'Ouse's silent tide'.

The church has suffered from fire and rather harsh restoration, but it has many interesting features, among them one of the finest memorial brasses in the County.

Autumn 1948

Bernard B West 1948

CALDECOTE – House Farm

One can only speculate on the original character of the new somewhat non-descript landscape between the romantic pine-clad oasis of Old Warden, Ickwell and Southill, where the Greensand influences both the natural and the built environment, and the open country to Biggleswade and beyond. Once it must have been rather grand, always intensely agricultural – the geology sees to that – but with individual buildings or isolated groups punctuating the landscape, rather than as at present forming a straggling and incoherent adjunct to it. Caldecote gives a glimpse here and there of settlement around former grazing areas, as at Home Farm where former common land is now a beautifully maintained 'green'. The rest is however a suburban picture with glimpses in the gaps of wooded hinterland towards Old Warden.

This was inevitable, of course. First came housing for the agricultural worker, related to the demands of the London markets and sited near the smallholdings where the labour was concentrated. The gaps left, interpreted in contemporary planning jargon as infill, produced the present pattern. One sees it from Blunham in the north, south to Langford and Clifton, and mostly it is not very attractive.

Caldecote House Farm was an early 19th-century precursor, undoubtedly associated with the Napoleonic wars and the contemporary agricultural expansion, but still put up at a time when the principles of Georgian propriety had not been relinquished. If only the present excellent maintenance went hand in hand with a tin of white paint. Green never works on buildings, except perhaps in its darkest shades, and least of all with gault brick. The porch is delightful, reminding one of the *tour de force* of trellising in Kimbolton High Street. House Farm porch has some gothic elements which contrast with the classical severity of the bay windows either side.

The green, newly mown in the spring first cut, is very attractive; it is only a pity that the Farm is alone in doing full justice in the setting.

Summer 1991

CAMPTON – Rectory Road

Estate cottages of the late 19th century form the centre of this most attractive range. These are a legacy of the Osborns' latter years when much of the village was rebuilt to an attractive rather chalet style with wide projecting eaves. In this case, however, we have a version of Victorian gothic with most attractive bargeboards and finials, the windows correctly if incongruously supplied with bold label moulds. Presumably, when this block was built the little 18th-century cottage next door received a porch to match: now derelict, it will be a serious loss to the road if this delightful little building is allowed to deteriorate into complete ruin.

The damage which can be brought about by replacement glazing is perfectly exemplified by this Victorian version of the 'semi-detached'. To the right the original fenestration survives, to the left single lights have been substituted with clumsy night vents and the character of the building is sadly marred. The glazing of the porch is also particularly nasty, fitted with narrow reeded bathroom glass, compared with the wholly appropriate trellis and planting of its neighbour where the character of the building is enhanced.

Much of the rest of Campton has been altered in character by new building but most of it is sensitive and well endowed with tree cover. There is one thatched range and one or two 17th-century survivors. All Saints, mostly of sandstone, is suspiciously smartened: there was a major restoration in 1898 but internally it retains, somewhat surprisingly, quite a lot 14th-century woodwork, particularly under the tower a screen in two light divisions. The Manor House is the one set piece; built in 1591 it has a long symmetrical front with five gables and a central porch. The rectory is plain, of the mid-18th century; it verges on being a rather gaunt building, but is important in giving the centre of the village some urbanity.

Autumn 1985

CARDINGTON

Of all the villages close to Bedford, Cardington can surely rank as the most unspoiled. Biddenham, although still an entity, is becoming suburban; and Elstow, though it survives almost miraculously, suffers from being on a main road and from the tide of raw building lapping it on the north. Although rather scattered, Cardington remains a village. Our 18th-century forebears endowed it with fine trees, now mature. Some of the elms on the green and in the churchyard were felled a year or so ago; but personally I have adjusted myself to their disappearance.

An almost indefinably aristocratic air is the village's great charm, a quality shared by other villages in mid and east Bedfordshire – the impression of being at the door of some great country house. Such an atmosphere requires continuous maintenance. Considering its proximity to the town, it is surprising that Cardington has not become a 'high-class residential area'.

St. Mary's church is, as the Victoria County History says, an unnecessary rebuilding (in 1898–1902). Although good in detail it is only the survival of the chancel and some of the Gascoigne tombs that save it from being merely a competent piece of Victorianism.

Of Cardington's links with history it is sufficient to mention that John Howard lived there for several years (Howard House is still an adornment to the village), and in the new churchyard is a monument not only to brave men but also to an idea that formed a checkered part in the story of man's conquest of the air. To one of my generation it seems a long time ago that the great airship R 101 passed over at night on its fatal journey, but in spite of all that has happened since, the stunning impact of the following morning's news is still a vivid memory.

Summer 1955

Cardington. May 1988.
Gerald Millet.

CARLTON

Of all the fictions surrounding the study and appreciation of landscape, those associated with deserted villages and isolated churches are probably the most commonplace, unless surpassed by the 'secret tunnel' folklore which is also inexplicably universal. At Carlton and Chellington, the Black Death is accepted in popular belief as the main cause for the isolation of the churches, particularly in the latter case. Most likely, however, is that both communities gravitated to the bridgehead at Harrold where exposure of limestone at a fairly shallow angle gave rise to an early ford and later, even probably in Roman times, the foundation for a bridge.

All the same any natural disaster, and that of the 1340s was undoubtedly the worst, must have hit hard, forcing the survivors into greater cooperation. Sadly the agricultural depression of 100 years later didn't help matters, and many a deserted village site owes its state to this, rather than the more easily comprehended plague.

Chellington, elevated above the river, is of course the more romantic, particularly with its monument to a former shepherd boy made good, Sir Robert Dawling, whose tomb now lies vandalised, forgotten and neglected. Nevertheless, St. Mary's at Carlton has something which Chellington lacks: parochial use. St. Mary's is still a living church, dignified by its isolation rather than being a melancholy landmark.

The surrounding Scots pines are at the limit of their lifespan – could one or two replacements be put in as they are now so much part of the character of the place? They set off the little church to perfection. St. Mary's must have had Saxon origins; only a little herring-bone masonry on the north side of the chancel can be used as proof, but it is enough. One interesting detail: there was obviously once a one bay south chapel, with traces on the wall of a priest's house and living room on the first floor. One forgets how in the early years 'living over the shop' was not unusual, only later came the *prieste house*, ancestor of our later vicarages and rectories.

Carlton-cum-Chellington is a well served community, the main road and Carlton High Street acting as two spines. Sensible infilling has contributed to its well-being, rather than detracted from it, but the most important characteristic is that there are clean edges all round, open country starts abruptly. Much as one derides Planning policies at times, this is one of the successes of control.

Autumn 1995

Carlton St Mary's
June 95. Bernard Welch F.I.S.A.

CLIFTON – Church of All Saints

This little church is a characteristic mid-Bedfordshire building on a small but dignified scale. It shows clearly in its building materials its dependence on County geology, for sandstone, limestone and the famous, but poorly-weathering Totternhoe stone, are to be found in the fabric.

The main work shown in the illustration is mid-14th century of that period known as Decorated, of which the east window with its reticulated or net tracery is a particularly glorious example. Actually the term Decorated is sometimes misleading, for numerous country churches of this period are very plain, the window tracery being the only guide to the date. The description applies more particularly to the great churches as, for example, Selby, Southwell Minster chapter house, Ely Cathedral Lady Chapel and so on, although at Wymington Bedfordshire has one small but very rich example of the style.

Clifton church, in company with many others, has not escaped the building zeal of the 19th century, and the work of enlargement in the north aisle is of a barbarity that shouts against the quiet dignity of the rest of the building. Victorian 'restoration' must have been terrifyingly thorough to anyone who loved their church, as a glance at gaunt skeletons undergoing treatment as shown in old prints and photographs will confirm. Caddington and Elstow come to mind as examples and unfortunately there are many more. So devastating were these 'restorations' that we can say now that the poorer the parish then usually the richer is its heritage.

Winter 1949

Bernard De West

CLOPHILL – Clophill House and Mill

The whole length of the High Street from the Green to the church and old rectory contains subject matter for a thousand drawings. Some infill has been inappropriate, some even disastrous, but the whole sequence is delightful and should be walked to benefit from the unexpected lateral views over walls, up alleyways and into gardens.

The fact that the river plays so little part in the scene is obviously because its benefits are privately enjoyed and in the Mill House gardens developed to something approaching classical landscape around the millhead. It is only at the mill itself downstream that the water rushes out of a miniature Piranesian cavern, all dark mossy masonry, as a podium to the lovely brickwork of the mill itself above, and is for once both visible and audible in the middle of the village. This is a grand little corner giving a fine setting for Clophill House across the road. All the more unbelievable, therefore, is the suburban mannerism to the south, including a house with silly barley sugar columns. All this contrasts sadly with simple dignified brickwork of House and Mill, when really good modern design could have contributed positively to the group. The House gains a lot from its decoration of urns and one marvellous pineapple. They may not all belong to the original design – one has a sneaking suspicion that they are of various periods – but the total effect is eminently satisfactory, particularly the two fine swagged specimens on the parapet. The only serious quibble one has with the elevation is the soil pipes. If ever it were possible to lose these in an internal duct, the benefit to an otherwise perfect building would be immense.

Summer 1981

Clophill House and Mill
March 1981
Edmund West

COCKAYNE HATLEY

The approach to St. John's is a little intimidating today, not really any longer in an orchard but almost in a garden, and that embedded in a large estate on a private road.

The site is magnificent, on the edge of the plateau, still capped by the old fragment of former forest cover in Potton Wood, with wide views into Cambridgeshire, the distant Gog Magog Hills closing the view. It is here just to the east that one has the great surprise of finding the chalk on the left, to the north, as well as in its usual relationship running with the southern horizon. The swell of the plateau edge to the left of this view is the prelude to this unexpected line of hills. To visualise now a huddle of streets and houses, with views out down alley-ways and over garden walls to this fine sweep of landscape, today again virtually unenclosed as it must have been in the Middle Ages, is not easy, so completely has the old settlement gone.

The village must have had some prosperity in the middle years of the 15th century, not a period noted for stable agriculture, but here there may have been sheep, due to the unexpected proximity of the chalk. Certainly, resources allowed a lavish west tower, compared for example with the standard Home Counties job at nearby Potton. The ogee-headed double belfry lights are highly competent shop work of the period for example. It always seems amazing that with a capacity for such precision in design, symmetry did not particularly preoccupy the mediaeval mason. On the north face of the tower, the stair turret pushes the belfry lights out of centre and one is reminded of other distressing examples such as at Whissendine in Rutland. The use of sandstone gives the tower tremendous character but probably makes it a bit more bucolic, and less sophisticated than its builder intended.

The fact that fine buildings in the Low Countries at Ghent, Louvain and Malines were robbed of their fittings to adorn St. John's was probably a matter of Henry Cust saving them from destruction, consequent on the same misguided reordering of church interiors as desecrated much of Wren's work in London, but they do not belong here and are even more incongruous than the lumber rooms similar taste has made of Pavenham and Old Warden churches.

Autumn 1981

Cockayne Hatley June 18' 1981.
Bernard West.

COLMWORTH – Church of St. Denis

A straightforward description of the church of St. Denis at Colmworth would fail to disclose the actual refinement of the building which has all the precision one expects of the late 15th century but which is seldom combined at that period with restraint. There was a time when it was fashionable to look upon any design after the plague years of the later 1340s as decadent and a pale shadow of the glories of the preceding two decades. Certainly, there was an understandable loss of exuberance in the later years of the fully developed 'Perpendicular' style, but it is rather the invention and elegance which surprises considering, with hindsight, how imminent and inevitable was the coming storm. Colmworth is the perfect example, and a rare one, of a village church in which the hand of a bold and individual designer can be discerned in every detail; it was built in four years from 1426 for Sir Gerald Braybrook, who was well served by his sadly anonymous architect.

The tower and spire are standard but with a subtle individuality, particularly in the spire; for example, the lucarnes face the cardinal points which is fairly unusual but the two rings are interesting with the topmost light enriched like a miniature corona. Aisleless, the interior is wonderfully light and consistent in detail: one wonders if the glass and woodwork were equally sophisticated. One angel only has survived in one of the north windows – hardly sufficient to gain any idea of former glories.

The monument to Sir William Dyer, erected by his wife in 1641, is notable in design. The caryatids at the base, Faith, Hope and Charity, are figures of some refinement for the period, and the famous if poignant epitaph of the 'widow bride' still evokes immediate sympathy even after 300 years.

In spite of infilling there is still a remoteness about Colmworth, but one has only to look at the denuded surrounding landscape, and compare it with maps of the village a mere 40 years ago, to realise how hedge removal has made a desert of its setting. The 'set-aside' or fallow grant of the recently revised agricultural policy is hardly attractive to grain farmers in this area at £80 an acre, and would not be much more so at £100, but some reduction in cultivation might mean that a few trees might again have the chance of survival to maturity even if only along the roads. Areas of small commercial woodland would even be a compensation on this now sadly bleak plateau.

Spring 1989

Colmworth. October 88
Berwick West. R.I.Br.A

COPLE – Church of All Saints

For the antiquarian, the interest of All Saints' church is its richness in
memorial brasses. That to Sir Walter Luke and his wife, Anne Launcelyn, is
probably the most interesting, especially for the use of pewter inlay in its
heraldic detail. The church itself, however, is a particularly compact and
unified little structure. Restoration has been reasonably restrained, though
there is peculiar detailing in the very East Anglian south porch which looks
like a combination of 18th-century meddling and 19th-century restoration.
Nevertheless, the porch is impressive and could easily be the entrance to
some grand 'wool church' in Norfolk. As one might expect from the geological
position of the village, the building is of stone, partly from the Ouse valley
and partly from the Greensand hills. It is unusual to see the normally rather
unreliable sandstone used for quoining in the tower.

Outside the attractive churchyard wall the village is rather disappointing.
Many of its buildings are simple and not without merit, but the central garage
which dominates the wide street is disastrous. Oil and petrol advertising is
generally aggressive and, although this display is not on the largest scale, the
street cannot absorb it. Yet the garage buildings have been and could again
become attractive. The road leading to Willington is irredeemable suburbia
and the same must be said for the south side of the Cardington road; but
some of the 'ends' are still unspoiled. It is to be hoped that they will be missed
by the speculator's roving eye; if there is to be considerable development
it should be controlled by a single architect (the centre of Felmersham is
an excellent example of a unified scheme) and not given over to the sort of
architectural 'free for all' of varying roof pitches and colours as, for instance,
the west end of Church Road at Willington.

Summer 1963

Cople May. 1963. Bernard West.

COTTON END – Herring's Green

Described as mid-18th century with 17th-century work elsewhere, one assumes that this fine farmhouse is a rebuilding of one of the holdings of the early enclosures that took place in the former pastoral country of the Bedford plain. Here and there such original buildings survive, but mostly they are complete late Georgian or 19th-century replacements.

This house appears on the 1794 Estate Map and one would have thought that it was of such importance that it would have had a more eminent status as a listed building, than just being on the supplementary list. This is undoubtedly one of the cases where a new evaluation of the building is needed, and one which finally and effectively protects it in a way which reflects its quality.

The entrance porch has been tinkered into a rather doubtful structure; one could have wished for a no-nonsense recognisable door case and fanlight or a porch with all the evidence of a proper pedigree but what there is, though a trifle thin, is plausible enough. The curved or Dutch gables, matched elsewhere in the County only at Woburn, form an architectural feature over which there is some controversy. Whether the influence of Dutch 17th- and 18th-century design was extensive in East Anglia generally is not as easy to establish as one tends to accept. The stepped gables of the Willington Dovecote, one can parallel throughout Brabant for example, and Henry Bell's Custom House at King's Lynn would sit well in the Hague, but by what route these influences arrived and to what degree they are truly Dutch is perhaps debatable. There was more possibly a common approach to a northern form of the Baroque spirit on both sides of the North Sea, but only in Holland did it approach the exotic in such situations as Broek in Waterland, or the local costume of the Zuyder Zee, under the direct influence perhaps of colonial connections.

The small corner of the plain to the south of Bedford is eminently precious. As its great elms fall one by one of necessity to combat disease which must surely reach epidemic proportions after another mild winter, one sees the landscape for what it is, fragile and dependent on the escarpment to the south for identity with the woods as relief. If brick-making ever spreads this far east to the broad landscape below Sheerhatch, for example, it will be a disaster. We should have ceased to build in brick before that becomes necessary but, depend on it, it will be in another material with a price to be paid in landscape loss.

Summer 1972

Hennings Green Cotton End
Kenneth Bristow April 1972

CRANFIELD

Suburban Cranfield to the north of the village and the airfield to the south-west are no introduction to what is still an attractive central area. As soon as one is away from the sterile uniformity of the housing which has had to conform to the building regulations and the County Surveyor's road requirements, there is just enough left of the casual and the picturesque grouping of an older Cranfield to make a few hundred yards of the middle of the place visually quite rewarding.

The actual centre of war memorial, shelter and landscaping suffers as do all centres from being the teenage 'stamping ground' and is well-vandalised, and strewn with litter but, if one can turn from all this too typical phenomenon, there are compensations. The *Carpenters' Arms*, for example, is a late Georgian building of the most perfect proportions and refinement, typical of so many like it in the centre of the County, and of a form which carried on almost without change of detail right into the 19th century. The little shop alongside, with a gay almost continental canopy, extends from the façade of a much older building, and is offset to the south by a new group of maisonettes, set in the old way, gable end to the street, with entrances along the length in porches for privacy. A nice piece of planning but coarsely detailed.

The break through to the east and the main green is made perfect by the island of buildings to the north, a pity only that the other pub is so urban and out of scale. The school however is great fun with an unlikely spirelet and some wonderfully wayward detailing.

Whatever happens to Cranfield with the inevitable pressures from Milton Keynes, infill or replacement in the centre must maintain present building lines and the number of mature trees which give the place so much of its charm at the moment.

Autumn 1974

DUNSTABLE

The centre of Dunstable, at the crossing of the Icknield Way and the Roman Watling Street, nowadays belies its antiquity. One recalls Worthington G. Smith's drawing of it before the days of the car and I can remember something of its character surviving until the immediate pre-war years when the dreadful suburban tentacle from the west side of Luton began to engulf the old town. High Street North keeps a little of its character, particularly around the *Sugar Loaf Hotel* of 1717, a memory of coaching days. Opposite there is a good 17th-century gateway, well restored, with round arch and columns and a gabled upper floor of brick with mullioned windows.

It is however High Street South which, in spite of the blocks of flats, preserves something of the character of old Dunstable, and of course the rich tree planting is a great help. The Priory House has a handsome early Georgian façade, with arched windows. The Cart almshouses of c. 1723 come next, a two-storied row of blue and rubbed brick in a rich red that makes the usual effective colour combination, and the Chews Grammar School of 1719. This is an exquisite, almost toy-like, building of perfect proportions, with a steep pediment and a delightful attenuated cupola. A five bay design of two stories, it has the extra ornament of little figures of charity children over the central door.

This is the character of the better Chiltern towns – Wendover, Amersham, Beaconsfield – which Dunstable has lost. All of them have been under siege for years, however, and I am reminded of H. J. Massingham in his *Chiltern Country*, where he speaks of suburbanisation – 'suburbia, so familiar, so little analysed, the culmination of an historical process reaching back to the Industrial Revolution, and beyond to the series of causes which made England abandon the ideal of self-subsistence for that of economic expansion.' Dunstable is a monument to the result of this process, which has in a sense deserted its old town life to betray the country around it. One is therefore thankful for any reminders of an age which, lacking our amenities and opportunities, nevertheless had some gentility.

There are indications that we have learnt lessons from the dreadful mistakes of the 1960s, that we are discovering a new urbanity, but it is a bit late for Dunstable to benefit.

Spring 1995

Dunstable Jan 9th '93
Bernard Web. F.I.E.A.

DUNTON

One needs to step across the road to enjoy the *March Hare* as a building; its enjoyment as a pub presents no problems, indeed the success of this particular house is well deserved. As the *Wheatsheaf* it was a rebuilding of the 1920s of remarkable sensitivity – canted to a curve in the road with an elaborate porch placed asymmetrically, it perpetuates the original layout of a central pub sandwiched between a cobbler's to the east and to the west two cottage shops, selling harness and bacon respectively. The name is new and is perhaps a little aggressively handled in panels scattered over the elevation, but colour and lettering are both chosen with care.

Overshadowing all this is Browning's 1861 rebuilding of the church tower, which, incorporating a substantial element of the original mediaeval stair turret, may be a restoration based on sound archaeological evidence. It is just that it does not quite look like it, though there are of course many precedents for the elongated belfry light. The masonry and details have a machine-made look, and it is perhaps this which is so unmediaeval in feeling.

St. Mary's has suffered from the use of chalk in its construction, and it seems likely that the material here is the notorious Melbourn stone from Cambridgeshire which seems to break up even more readily than Totternhoe stone, particularly externally. There is some fine and slightly wayward window tracery of the late 14th century, particularly in the east window which anticipates the vertical lines of the next century, but built, as much of it is, again in chalk. Total external replacement will soon be the only option.

At the centre of Dunton is this pub and church island, it is a pity that on the south side the old people's homes make only a small contribution to any sense of enclosure. The conversion of the chapel is heartless, and terraces both to north and south are not strong enough in scale to hold the view together. However, one cannot praise the estate on the north-east corner too highly. Here the use of weather boarding and pantiles has caught an echo of the original *genus loci* and exploited it superbly.

Autumn 1983

EATON BRAY

Bedfordshire's share of the Vale of Aylesbury, lying mostly to the west of the A5 and south of Billington Hill, is saved only by its southern hinterland of hills, in particular the magnificent profile of Ivinghoe Beacon.

As a County we have worse body sores than Eaton Bray, but the spreading tattiness is unbearable in what is still a semi-rural setting. Tilsworth suffers from it, so do parts of Totternhoe and Stanbridge, and one wonders how and why the much vaunted planning control of the last thirty years has so utterly failed to hold these villages of the plain in some sort of order. Certainly, the pattern of settlement, even before the Enclosures, was scattered, with higher density and roadside development only near the older centres of church and manor, as at Tilsworth. Thus a case for infilling could always be made, with a result which now amounts to little more than sprawl. What is so dreaful, however, is the proliferation of bleak housing estates planted without land-scaping or the least consideration for surviving older buildings.

The Rye, a moment of order and decency in a sea of suburbia and silly Disneyesque conversions, is therefore something to be treasured. The bleak sports pavilion, cheaply built and poorly maintained, with a pot-holed car park, is only too typical to the north; so as usual one needs blinkers to take in the prospect. Whatever will become of this part of the County! There is still so much to enjoy, but it cannot take many more years of this treatment, before we have a sort of miniature Middlesex from Hockliffe to Northill.

One can begin to understand the blinkered ecclesiologist or pure anti-quarian, who seeks out the incomparable carving in St. Mary's and turns his back on the rubbish outside. How to understand, let alone tolerate, the house opposite in which one can still distinguish the bones of a comfortable yeoman's house of the early 17th century? What tortured mind (resorting one supposes to the pages of all the available 'glossies') could so distort history, and create the dreadful caricature which now passes for a half-timbered house?

Thus St. Mary's is the reservoir of older values, of an age as remote from us as the art of the stonemason from that of the computer programmer. Is it more valid, does it stand for something atavistic, lost now to the technician with his social mobility, polishing his car outside? Perhaps art and science have gone their separate ways and this is the real dichotomy. We ought to think about the effects even if we cannot resolve the problem, because the landscape is the casualty.

Spring 1980

EDWORTH

From the A1 a wide grassy approach to Manor Farm and church is a promise of the incomparable setting of these buildings, slightly down a south-easterly slope but with wonderful views southwards to the chalk hills. Today, with the church in isolation, and almost reduced to the scale of a garden ornament by the giant trees, it is difficult to visualise its original state as the centre-piece of a huddle of cottages on the edge of the hill. The scatter of houses that is present day Edworth is the typical survival pattern of yeoman farms or holdings dispersed from the old peasant community, with the Manor itself becoming the typical Manor Farm of post-enclosure prosperity in the early 19th century. This a handsome house, typical in its large windows and deep hipped roof, but the more recent extensions in a genteel garden city idiom belong to a suburban Home Counties tradition.

St. George's, long neglected, is undergoing repair, and some reduction by removal of battlements. Such repair is now almost Diocesan policy; witness the painful skyline of nave and aisles at St. Peter's, Thurleigh. But faced with the alternative of demolition what does one do? The writer was forced to mutilate T. Smith's St. Mary's, Clophill, for the same reason, but the architectural loss is considerable and especially so when, as here at Edworth, the string course on the porch is of necessity the prop to a tight-fitting lid, this being a more appropriate term than roof. With some removal of dreadful cement render, texture is being brought back to the building, the use of tiles to strengthen quoins is delightful, and always the cobbles or, more properly, boulder clay erratics make an attractive wall surface.

As for the landscape, we see here one of the last really great stands of elm in the County but, as last January at Dean, for how long? One is aware that some members of the agricultural community would fell the last tree in the British Isles if it shaded a Brussels sprout, but such extreme attitudes are not universal, and both the farming Smyths of Edworth are to be congratulated on their landscape, which is no accident. The irony will be grim if this is the last season that these trees survive: there were signs of disease last summer in several.

Spring 1976

EGGINGTON HOUSE

Eggington House was probably built as early as 1694, possibly for one Renouille, a French merchant tailor of the Languedoc district, who arrived in this country during the reign of William and Mary. Suggestions that he was assimilated locally so quickly as to become County sheriff within a few years are difficult to confirm. In 1728 Joseph Carter prepared a plan of the estate for John Reynal, which is undoubtedly Renouille in an anglicised form. At that time the house was in the occupation of Richard Gurney, which makes one wonder if it was built later than traditionally supposed or whether it was built for one of the Andrews family at the earlier date and later modified. John Reynal was dead by 1738, and his son, John James Reynal of Lincoln's Inn, who had obtained a grant of arms in 1737, inherited. He died in 1767. The only definite record of a sheriff of Bedfordshire from this family was John Sayer Neal Renal (apparently he had dropped the 'y') in 1777.

Architecturally, an interesting point is that a deep wooden cornice seems to have been replaced by the present panelled parapet, probably between the years 1694 and 1728, and Carter illustrates the house with three urns on the skyline. These were subsequently removed but the present owner has replaced the central urns and added two more, which gives the silhouette of the house, just the extra interest it needs. There appears to be no records of architect or builder, but it is good provincial work of the period which any local man could have realised from the pattern books of the day.

Today the house and its estate are beautifully maintained. Sophisticated and scholarly restoration has done much to enrich not only the building but also its surroundings. It has remained for one of the public authorities to insert a particularly heartless intrusion into the scene, and I have omitted the telegraph poles from my drawing. Had they been included they would have completely dominated the most satisfactory aspect of the house as seen from outside the grounds. Bedfordshire displays many dreadful examples of insensitive siting of poles, but this is probably one of the most uncouth.

Autumn 1964

Eggington August 1964 Bernard B West.

ELSTOW – Moot Hall and Church

Over the years, in drawing for the *Bedfordshire Times*, and since 1947 for the *Bedfordshire Magazine*, there have been certain stock views one has tended to avoid, not because their merit is in any way in doubt but because they are inevitably so hackneyed. Elstow abounds in such views, many of them as picturesque as they ever were, but it does not do to look closely. The immediate centre with its Bunyan associations, the Moot Hall and the church, is fine and dignified, but the surroundings show signs of dereliction which are disconcerting. Things have gone in recent years which one regrets: Bunyan's cottage though of dubious antiquity, and constantly battered by traffic, should never have disappeared. It was a pity it could not survive until the by-pass. The loss of the cottages by the vicarage meant the disappearance of a strong horizontal emphasis set against the church tower, which as a composition was just right. One dreads the possibility that we might have a fancy dress parade of neo-Georgian here which could be out of scale.

Full rehabilitation and the removal of pebble dash would do wonders for Elstow, infilling to keep the place alive and lavish tree planting. The epidemic of elm disease has been a dreadful event for the village, particularly to the south of the church where the skyline is certainly saved by the magnificent sycamore behind the ruins.

However, it is a by-pass which will save the place. To sit drawing near to the A6 is to await the sound of impact after every squeal of brakes. People leaving the *Red Lion* do so on the outside of a curve near a dangerous junction, and no one seems to slow down. The miracle is that accidents and damage to buildings are not daily occurrences.

Winter 1973

EVERSHOLT

Place-names which commemorate extinct wild animals are not common. In Eversholt we have 'the wood of the boar' or *eofors-holt*, from the Old English *eofor*, which has become *eber* in modern German. In the well tended Bedfordshire countryside it seems a far cry to the days when this ugly and sometimes dangerous animal was wild, but even today the deep woodland around Woburn could still support it. The ecology of the district differs little from that of some of the woodlands in the Teutoburger forest of North Germany, where, on one occasion, I was glad enough to shin up a tree for safety from an enraged member of the species.

Eversholt is one of our loveliest villages. Though scattered, it has kept its identity. Its atmosphere is that of a long Victorian summer's afternoon, which is undisturbed by the mild anomaly of some good Georgian building and an austerely perfect little early 19th-century house by the church. Perhaps this area and its counterpart around Old Warden appealed to the scenic standards of the Victorian era; it is so reminiscent of the coloured postcards of the 1860s.

The simple structure of the church of St. John the Baptist retains 14th-century work in the chancel but in the main is an unadventurous 15th-century example saved from the mediocrity by its pleasant building material and the refinement of its porch in which the sophistication of the age has triumphed over what must have been a fairly tight budget. The Collyweston slates of the chancel roof come as a surprise; they are modern – part of Scott's restoration. Quite likely they were ordered jointly with those for Turvey, which he dealt with about the same time. The Victorians saw no particular desirability for the use of regional materials, or even local style for that matter, witness the Northamptonshire spire at Ridgmont.

Winter 1956

Eversholt September 86. Bernard Field

EYEWORTH – Church of All Saints

By all accounts, and particularly from that of John Kendall at Church Farm, the storm of 20 September 1967 that wrecked the spire of All Saints', Eyeworth, had all the characteristics of those scarcely credible visitations of the 17th century when the skies were full of dreadful portents, strange lights and sounds. Certainly, the hard evidence of electric points and plugs exploding off the walls cannot be questioned, nor perhaps the stories of St. Elmo's fire, an unmistakable phenomenon. The progress of a large manifestation of ball lightning, finally exploding on the spire, does however stretch the imagination although there are numerous such records, and indeed something similar happened at Eyeworth in the 1890s.

The loss of the spire was tragic. It was slightly out of place from the normal area of distribution of spires and important as such, and its position on the ridge of value out of all proportion to its size. Bingham Harris's bell cote has a slight whiff of Butterfield, rather like the end of one of those 19th-century school chapels where the endowment ran out, but this is probably a jaundiced reflection on the loss of former elegance. Someday, if funds ever permit, a fanciful scrolly weather-vane on the turret would work wonders.

The rehallowing of the tower took place on 6 November 1970 and was carried out by Robert Runcie, when Archbishop of Canterbury. This was after the church had been ransacked by vandals, and brasses and even one of the bells stolen.

After the elegance and tangible prosperity of Sutton and a pleasant approach along a fine belt of oaks, the climb to Eyeworth ridge is a disappointment. The village straggles along the road and is the one place where one or two compact doses of good quality infilling would give a new vitality, together with intensive tree planting. It is hard today to visualise the fine house and estate of the Andersons now all utterly swept away, and there is an undeniable bleakness which nevertheless could be ameliorated.

Summer 1984

Eyeworth Church April 5ᵗʰ 84

FARNDISH

The Nene valley villages of north-west Bedfordshire, Podington, Farndish and Wymington, must once have been remote indeed. Before the expansion of the 'boot and shoe' towns even Wymington would have been compact and low lying in its valley.

Only Farndish perfectly preserves this sense of isolation, although the red ramparts of Woolaston are slightly menacing on the skyline. All the Northamptonshire ingredients are here: the rich ironstone, symbol of the 19th-century devastation of so much of our neighbouring county; limestone everywhere, with the familiar masonry details, deriving from Cotswold tradition; finely detailed stacks and mullioned windows. Only the Collyweston slates have disappeared in my lifetime – here they were just about at their southern most limits, costly to replace and on the few buildings where one remembers them, already badly decayed and slipping after the neglect of the war years.

The village, however, is perfect, consisting of a combination of fine isolated buildings rather than composing into an actual street like Podington, and the church is little more than another barn in scale. Its details, however, elements in simple walling, all unrelated to each other, lift it to the sort of sculptural level that made its retention after redundancy of the greatest importance. The south door is probably the favourite architectural detail in the County, 13th-century work relying on an arch of alternating brown and grey stone instead of mouldings, and strangely evocative of Moorish detail. It is not, of course, entirely far fetched to see Saracenic influence in some early Gothic detail: the emotional impact of the Crusades had some strange side-effects, and nowhere was too remote for them to penetrate.

Autumn 1977

Farndish. July 4th 1977.

FELMERSHAM – Church of St. Mary

Begun in 1220, the same year as Salisbury Cathedral, Felmersham Church was carried through to completion in some twenty years, and it still retains much of its lovely Early English architecture.

Apparently the original intention of the builders was to complete the tower with a stone spire – the rough stones for a squinch arch to hold it can be seen in the angles of the first stage above the roof. However, in the 14th century the tower was carried up a further stage and a stair turret added. The square silhouette which results marries very happily with the flat 15th-century roof, more so perhaps than a spire would have done. The 15th-century nave roof was made by raising high walls above the nave arcades and piercing them with clerestory windows to light the interior, the whole being covered with a fairly flat timber roof with lead on the outside. All this alteration in no way interfered with the earlier west front, except of course that the gable was lowered. For the apex they reused the fine 13th-century cross.

The interior is very fine, especially under the great arches of the central tower, but it disappoints a little, probably because of some really bad Victorian glass and some very unfortunate fittings – the reredos is an outstanding example of bad taste. Little angel crockets are carved around the central arch of the 15th-century screen, a wonderful survival. It retained its gallery until the middle of the last century when it perished, doubtless on one of the current Victorian pretexts as either superfluous or unsafe.

A perfect setting high above the road and overlooking the River Ouse enhances the beauty of the west front towering above the observer. See it in spring when the daffodils are in flower above the old churchyard wall and the great chestnut trees on the south side are in bud – a lovely frame to a lovely church.

Autumn 1950

FLITTON

Compared with its neighbour villages, Flitton is slightly 'off the map', Flitwick (with a name also derived from the river on which they both stand) having a station on the main railway line, and Silsoe, carved out of the old Flitton parish in 1831, standing on a main road. The village has not so much spread as erupted in a scattered and haphazard westward development. But it is not lacking in charm where it is based around old cottage groups. The additions are often sympathetic and make tolerable the rather dense over-building. Travelling eastwards one plays the urban rather than the rural game of hide and seek with the church tower, elevated on its knoll pin-pointing the village centre, but only at the corner by the church does the pleasant visual effect break down. Chicken farms and smallholdings are not industries which many landscapes absorb easily, and when, as in front of one or two good views of the church, they appear partly derelict, the effect, aided by some really gross telegraph poles and a network of overhead wiring, is disastrous.

The little street behind the church, subject of the sketch, is quite delightfully 'old English'. The thatched cottages have an almost Wessex cosiness, with none of the East Anglian angularity that might be expected in this area. Apart from the fantastic and hideous de Grey mortuary chapel, the church is a typical, competent piece of work of about 1460–70. The chapel, architectural parasite on the little building, has the vaguely pagan air associated with the late 18th century, but was begun in 1614 and had taken its final form by 1705.

Spring 1958

FLITWICK
– Church of St. Peter and St. Paul

St. Peter and St. Paul, like so many churches in Bedfordshire, has lost its village. At Flitwick the road junction of Church End to the east was probably the original centre of the settlement, but with the coming of the railway the whole focus changed completely. Urban Flitwick is much more a southern continuation of Ampthill suburbs than a place with its own identity.

This central part of the County – Westoning, Flitwick, Flitton, Tingrith and Steppingley – is the sort of country that varies from the richly picturesque to the deadly dull in a matter of miles. One can travel on a bleak piece of road like that from Steppingley to Flitwick, arrive at the railway station with its attendant reminders of a nondescript outer London suburb, and then in a matter of half a mile discover Church End and the wooded grounds of Flitwick Manor.

Flitwick Church, a simple structure of the 13th to the 15th centuries, has undergone its share of Victorian falsifications but retains much of value, particularly its east window. Like many of the churches in the Greensand country, it is submerged in the trees of the estate planting of the last 150 years. Southill is an even better example. The Victorian ideal landscapes of evergreen, yews, pines, cypresses and laurels, picturesque though they are, can be overpowering. It is all magnificently sombre and luxurious, but ivy plays too important a part and there is always the impression of being in a cemetery or garden of rest. It is heretical to say so, but surely there is a feeling of relief as one emerges into the open country in which deciduous trees and arable farming predominate.

The lych-gate in my illustration is a grand specimen of the hearty carpentry that developed from the pattern of the few surviving mediaeval examples. Here it is acceptable because of its setting. Such is far from being the case in some other villages, where gross and elaborate structures ruin the dignity of the simple fabrics to which they form the entrance.

Winter 1960

Flitwick Church.
October. 60. Bernard B West

GREAT BARFORD

This characteristic stretch of river scenery, the water meadows at Great Barford, owes much of its beauty to the fine trees grouped along the fields on either side of the Ouse, and in particular to the line of Lombardy poplars now in their maturity which form a landmark along this part of the valley. They are a little irregular now through old age and gales but there are enough left to indicate the imaginative way in which they were planted so as to punctuate, when fully grown, the wide flat meadows with just the right vertical emphasis. The bridge in contrast emphasizes the breadth of the landscape. Its length of seventeen arches effectively ties the church and houses into a lovely picture of buildings and landscape in unity.

Basically, the bridge is of the 15th century but it has been much restored and widened, with brick arches built out on to the old stone cutwaters, and carried up as a brick parapet. The church has been completely rebuilt save for the 15th-century tower, a simple but very satisfactory example of its period.

Summer 1952

HARROLD – Bridge

Of all Bedfordshire bridges Harrold's is the most romantic. Its long causeway from Carlton, raised above winter floods, and the sinuous lines of the structure spanning the river, represent several centuries of adaptations and rebuilding. There is affinity between Harrold's parapets and the lovely structural lines of the canal bridges of the early 19th century; more than likely this is a consequence of rebuilding at that time. But much of the stonework and one arch built with Northamptonshire ironstone date from the mid-14th century. The ironstone arch is hidden in the drawing by the wall of the 'lay by' that breaks the main line of the bridge. The villagers have a tradition that the bridge is built on Roman foundations and incorporates Roman work; but this seems to me unlikely, even bearing in mind the proximity of Irchester, once a Roman settlement. If there was a trackway it would hardly have justified a permanent structure in those days, particularly at a point where the river must always have been fordable. Probably the not uncommon confusion between Roman and Norman work has been made: organisation of the river valley settlements after the Conquest, with a fairly dense population in the valuable water-meadow grazing lands, would make a bridge necessary. Some masonry of that period may survive but certain identification of it is nearly impossible.

We must, I suppose, expect a scheme for widening to be proposed sooner or later. While it is not difficult to widen an architectural unity like Bedford bridge, with a structure which appears to grow out of the landscape and follow its harmonies, and which derives its character from a patchwork of periods and the work of many different hands, the problem is, if not insurmountable, at least one that will inevitably bring censure on whoever tackles it. Fortunately, Harrold bridge does not carry a major road and may survive the tyranny of the motor vehicle into a future age of aerial transport. Or is the weekly helicopter to market and peace on the roads too fanciful a concept?

Winter 1954

HASELLS HALL

Heylock Lingsley bought Hasells Manor in 1721 and between then and his death in 1749 it is evident that he completely rebuilt the house. His daughter Elizabeth was apparently able to welcome her husband William Pym to the finished building by that date, and the general style of the house would confirm this.

It is a building of great subtlety and refinement and this has probably led to the assumption that William Pym enlarged or rebuilt that which his father-in-law had begun, and that the detail belongs more to the later years of the 18th century. However, the treatment of the fenestration, the use of the Doric order on the porch, the balustrading and the general profile of the mouldings seem to confirm a date in the 1740s but by a very assured hand, someone surely more sophisticated than a country builder. It would be interesting to know who was responsible, and research into building accounts and estate records might disclose the architect, if as seems likely there actually was one.

The interior is frankly disappointing, and institutional use has laid a heavy hand on the whole internal identity of the building, but the rooms are very well proportioned and if only a use could be found for the house it could come alive again. As it is the house is under sentence, taxation and the cost of maintenance being once again the agents of destruction. The estate and Mr. Pym himself will be and probably already have been handed out the platitudes of responsibility and inheritance, but the fact is that at a time when lip service is paid in government circles to environmental values, and when more appreciation and awareness of our heritage of fine buildings is evident than ever before, the burden of maintenance and repair is made yearly more intolerable. Grants of various kinds are available, and there must be many invidious choices between the merits of buildings to receive them but the fact is that the whole question of the worth of our architectural heritage needs fresh examination.

The listing of a building should be more of a protection than it is at the present, and should bring with it some form of relief or assistance. The owner is in a sense a custodian after all.

One can only hope that something like the use of the nearby Lodge could happen to Hasells. Its setting and its views are as fine or finer perhaps in some ways than the RSPB Headquarters, although lacking the wilder heathland character. But whoever wants the house and could put it to an economic use needs to be on the scene fairly quickly.

Winter 1971

Hasells Hall October 1971

HAYNES

Haynes or Hawnes (the Ordance Survey and popular usage seem to have decided on the former name) is a perfect street village with a real break between buildings and countryside at either end, a definition worth noting when the start and finish of so many villages are obscured by an indeterminate clutter of housing estates, allotments and filling stations. One hopes that planning control will maintain it. The village is quite satisfactory architecturally. Haynes Park, now Hawnes School, with its piquant contrast between the red brick west façade and the gault brick remainder, is largely the work of Thomas Ripley and was probably complete by 1720. Ripley was at one time chief carpenter to the Board of Works and his grand and massive staircase is evidence of his training. The rectory, a simple north-facing 18th-century house, has a fine doorcase unfortunately made nonsensical by a Victorian porch planted on it. Some of the cottages seem to date from the late 17th century or earlier. The example I illustrate, with typical massive chimney stacks, has been well restored and maintained, and has a fine enclosed garden.

Externally, the church is a grim little building with harsh Victorian window tracery and mechanical masonry details. Its so-called 'restoration' was in 1850 – a date which would tell one, even without a visit, that the fabric would be reduced to architectural sterility. Our Lady of Haynes retains some sensitive detailing inside, dating from the 14th and 15th centuries. The tower was spared the vicious treatment of the rest of the building, but as a whole its character has gone.

Autumn 1962

Haynes August. 1962. Bernard Well.

HEATH AND REACH

Heath and Reach is rather like the curate's egg, but luckily the parts that are good are very good indeed. A scattered community is always vulnerable to insensitive development and parts of this village should never have happened. Surroundings which fifty years ago must have been delightful are now carved up into numerous sandpits, creating Nash or Piper landscapes of strange, raw beauty amid the woodlands. Eventually, gorse and broom bring a return to a more natural appearance – but the process is a long one. Then there is the universal blight of wire. I have suppressed the fantastic effect of the numerous telegraph poles on the green in my illustration, but for really heartless siting that by the pump could not be equalled, and the effect of wires radiating from this central position ruins the perfect siting of the houses around the Green.

It is an area under constant threat; the London-Birmingham motorway is a factor that will inevitably bring radical alterations within twenty years, aided by improved rail services to Leighton Buzzard. The threat may not be on the scale of that to Middlesex, which was realised in dreadful terms during the 1920s and 1930s and obliterated a landscape, for surely we are wiser today; but pressure on land is increasing and some development already carried out is not a happy augury for the future.

The Green is a microcosm of village development through three centuries. The surviving half-timbered range of the mid-17th century flanked by a simple 18th-century range is offset by a perky little Victorian village pump that makes an ideal centrepiece. A really hideous feature is out of sight – an elephantine chapel of illiterate design as out of scale and character as only some Victorian chapels can be.

Summer 1961

Heath and Reach, May 1961. Bernard B. West.

HENLOW

Of the two corridor street villages by the Ivel, Langford and Henlow, the latter undoubtedly has the most charm. The main road, the A507, from Clifton to Stotfold, completely ignores what is unexpectedly one of the finest streets of continuously good and well maintained houses in east Bedfordshire. Starting at the church with its ingenious little Victorian shelter in the foreground and ending at the cross roads, one has a continuous variety of elevations to enjoy, of which those of the late 18th century are undoubtedly the finest.

Mulberry House has had the good fortune to be cared for and is considerably enhanced by the retention and excellent maintenance of trees on the road boundary. The fine stands of Scotch pines, for instance, at the north end of the garden have the same value in the street as the Holm Oak in St. John's, Bedford, although there the latter is the one thing that saves an otherwise desolate stretch; here the pines are an enrichment. In the long length of the frontage the boundary posts and chains stake a legal claim and with the bay windows are a piece of detail in just the right place.

One must hope that if any development off the 'corridor' ever takes place it will be done by feeder roads at right angles to the main street, retaining as far as possible the main elevations and neither replacing them nor occupying garden space parallel to the road. If a more sensible policy with regard to old building lines could be envisaged by the County Surveyor, there would be less of a threat for the future, but for purely arbitrary reasons a building with its front door on the pavement, like Mulberry House, would be impossible today. This mania for setting back produces that most useless commodity, the front garden, and that most dull of streets where there is no sense of enclosure and surprise.

Summer 1965

Mulberry House Henlow Bedfordshire
May 1965. Bernard OWest.

HINWICK HOUSE

The pleasant little trinity of Podington, Farndish and Wymington forms one of the most delightful corners of Bedfordshire. At Podington with Hinwick we get a glimpse of an older England where recent years of flux and despoliation have made surprisingly little impression; only Wymington is infected by the sprawl of nearby Rushden.

Hinwick House, in its little park, is a building of manageable proportions, not a vast, crumbling mediaeval complex, nor elephantine and coldly Palladian, but built in a period when the pure classical style was a new-found discipline capable of giving four-square clarity to the smaller English house, a clarity that at Hinwick 19th-century additions have only slightly marred. The house was started in February 1709 by Richard Orlebar. In all probability he was his own architect, for his building accounts make no mention of employing anyone to prepare a design, and by this time any competent master mason would have had the knowledge to prepare moulding and other details, even if he found overall design rather advanced. The Diana pediment is another indication of Richard's inspiration, in this case a husband paying a compliment to a well-loved wife by allegorical allusion to her as the ancient goddess of the chase. She was Diana, daughter of Sir Samuel Astry of Henbury, Gloucestershire, and the Astry arms impaled by Orlebar grace the delightful scroll-pedimented entrance door.

The Turret House is the old manor house with a clock tower dated 1710 added. The ground floor was used for farming livestock, and the family lived above on the first floor.

Winter 1959

Bernard BWest Hinwick October 1959.

HOCKLIFFE

'Enter His gates with thanksgiving and His courts with praise', or so it says in the church porch, but as with so many village churches today, the porch is as far as you can go. St. Nicholas is obviously another case of the sanctification of a pagan site, like Shillington, Billington and Edlesborough, by realistic and far-sighted early converts. This little knoll with its wonderful views westwards over the Vale of Aylesbury is just about perfect. Obviously the Lodge is the grandest house, a fine Georgian elevation in plum-coloured and red brick, which is a characteristic colour combination in the south of the County. The little cottage below the east end of the church, in a perfect setting, strikes the only discordant note. One day perhaps someone will be able to afford the rethatching it so desperately needs. The present red corrugated iron is really disheartening when everything else is so appropriately maintained.

As usual in this district the church has suffered from the poorly weathering properties of both Totternhoe stone and sandstone. Some of the refacing and new window tracery is a little heartless. However, the enlightened removal of Roman cement from the tower has been followed by careful making good and repointing. This is a treatment which could well be continued even if, as seems likely, it did actually start by accident probably in the extreme conditions of last winter.

The churchyard contains one or two graveboards to the north of the tower; much weathered and no longer decipherable. They are a relic of a time when in a district without a decent freestone it was too costly to import from the distant Cotswold or Charnwood Forest. One sees few of these now and soon the last will be gone, but they were a feature of the Chilterns and their foothills for much of the 18th and early 19th centuries.

Down Church Lane, Watling Street brings a harsh return to late 20th-century reality, and what this century has done to main road Hockliffe is unbelievable. Council housing at the bottom of the Lane is a bad start, the centre block in raw Flettons with scrofulous peeling stucco on gabled blocks either end.

On the main road fine Georgian ranges survive with the earlier former *White Horse Inn* still retaining some of its slightly pathetic fragments from Toddington Manor as decoration for the façade. On an E-plan, with the centre sprig a fine double bay, this is a building which needs care more than incidental embellishment. Up the hill an early 18th-century elevation has been decked out in 'painted on' half timber of a wayward assurance that would provide a good backdrop for Snow White and the Seven Dwarfs. Main road catering carries its attendant clutter, and Planning control has obviously 'washed its hands' and turned away. One appreciates all the more the solitude of Church End, the only fitting prelude to the concealed delights of central Buckinghamshire beyond.

Winter 1982

HOUGHTON CONQUEST

One is loyal and loving to one's native county, but such sentiments are strained to breaking point at times by the contemplation of scenes which cause a sinking of the heart. There are villages which I have missed or avoided and when I return I can understand why. To go to draw at Houghton Conquest is to realise that there are worse body sores on the face of the County but few so pathetic.

Only the incomparable Old Rectory, built by Zachary Grey in the 1730s during his incumbency, at the end of its avenue of ancient limes, gives us an echo of the older Houghton, of a village surrounded by the seats of minor gentry, whose vanished homesteads are only marked now by remote moats in the fields. The Rectory with its background of King's Wood and the line of the hills still has the ambience of a country seat, its style and dignity in strange contrast to the general meanness of Rectory Lane.

The evolution of such a village as this presupposes that till the late 18th century there would have been a considerable survival of half timber or wattle structures under tile or thatch. Conquest Bury was demolished in 1856, a fine half-timbered building which we would treasure today. We only have Fisher's 1820 watercolour by which to remember it. With the enclosures many inhabitants of the actual village would have been reduced to the level of a landless labouring class, virtual paupers. The survivors managed to colonise the long strips of 'waste' by the roads, and these slightly grim though still Georgian terraces, often with sadly mutilated glazing or partially ruinous, still exist on several frontages. The old cottages, flimsy around their sandstone or brick chimney stacks, did not survive those lean years before modern affluence to become the estate agents' ideal of a 'wealth of old oak beams'. So the outlines went hard in brick and Welsh slate, with only a pub or two maintaining any elevational character.

J.W. Burgon's condensed memoirs in the winter '73 issue of the *Bedfordshire Magazine* describe the decline of Houghton from a late 19th-century standpoint, and he dates it back to the Civil War. By the 1840s the church was all but forsaken. Decline continuing to our own day leaves the village a scrappy and bleak little place, redeemed only along the Grove (the name itself a memory of another lost house) by the very distinguished *Knife and Cleaver* and by well detailed housing which flanks it. The church, in spite of its vicissitudes, is all texture; even after much restoration the tawny sandstone contrasts with mouldering Totternhoe stone from which the cement patching has spalled to give the sort of wall faces which delighted the early topographical draughtsmen like Cotman and which must have been universal in their lifetime, just before restoration and after two centuries of neglect.

Restoration doubtless saved the building, but we would probably greatly treasure the interior today if it had survived with three-decker pulpit, Conquest pew and hour glass for monitoring sermons. Still, apart from the Old Rectory and the *Knife and Cleaver*, it is one building in the village to which the eye turns for relief, and for that we should be grateful.

Summer 1982

HULCOTE – Church of St. Nicholas

Elizabethan churches are a rarity and to see something as mediaeval in outline with a recorded building date of 1590 is to realise that the old forms died hard and that the County builder was capable well into the years of the 17th century of building in a passable Gothic manner. Richard Charnock, the builder of the church, died in 1615, three years before Inigo Jones started the building of the Queen's House at Greenwich, and four years before the Banqueting Hall, both Palladian, fully fashioned and understood. In fact, Gothic – of a kind – went on at places, like Oxford and Warwick, to a point where it is hard to distinguish survival from revival, and it is possible to conclude that as a style it has never been out of production, although Liverpool Cathedral could be its last grand fling.

The Charnocks seem to have come from Lancashire to Hulcote in 1541 and one can only ponder on the link that stimulated what for those days would have been a major journey. The first Richard Charnock died in 1549 so his sojourn in the Midlands was not long enjoyed. The builder of the church whose initials, proudly offset by studwork, adorn the porch door was his son. The churchyard is a tangle of nettles now with dense overgrown evergreens, but the really grand thing is the wide bosky lime avenue as an approach. Does this represent an original village street or a formal avenue to the farm which, pleasant though it is, is hardly an adequate termination?

Autumn 1970

Hulcote Church
July 1970.

HUSBORNE CRAWLEY

This is another of the Bedfordshire views which is likely to be a certainty for inclusion in any official guide, but is none the worse for that. In fact this westward sloping triangular green though beset by traffic is as satisfactory a piece of enclosed space as we have in the County. Only the corner to Aspley Guise is dominated by an amorphous and ill-sited barn and a house in construction, the emerging details of which do not exactly raise the spirits. The adjoining cottage to the north is newly restored and in fact the work is not yet complete. This will be the making of this whole composition, particularly as seen from the entrance to Manor Farm, and one rejoices to see the work stopping short of prettification. It is all good consolidation of a fine though long derelict late 17th-century range which one had always hoped would be saved.

To the east is the famous view, Manor Farm of the 1590s with a magnificent clustered stack and later fenestration, and the church tower with its unlikely dark green masonry rising behind. The later, sleek, hill hugging barns below the level of the churchyard, but graded up the slope above the road, are a perfect foil to the house which dominates them. It is only when one peers over the edge, as it were, to the north, that the desolation of Brogborough is seen for what it is – a tragedy, albeit a necessary one. Only to the south and the hills is the country which for Hoskins was 'unsurpassed in sanctity and peculiar purity', and that survives precariously. God knows what the proposed City Fantasia would do to it. If this project goes ahead, and we are to experience Disneyland, or as we are told the pleasure park as people really want it, then look at Husborne Crawley for the last time, on Ridgmont climbing its hill, or Lidlington where the still picturesque huddle of houses on this beleaguered escarpment speaks of a rural past. It is as badly mauled a landscape as any in its present condition but a mob takeover would finish it.

Predictable reactionary prejudice from a contributor to a conservative County magazine? Possibly; but from one who has studied in some depth the environmental disaster of the Englishman taking his pleasures, I have discovered that I am not yet able to accept the crass vulgarity which seems to be involved in pleasure catering. What the pits should have is a comprehensive plan for a new Lake District for 2074, from Elstow to Husborne Crawley and Cranfield to Cardington. All sorts of leisure activities would fit into such a project.

Spring 1974

Husborne Crawley
January 1974. Dennis B Webb

ICKWELL GREEN

This is our best example now of the big squared village, a settlement around a common grazing ground. In fact it is almost our only one, now that the centre of Felmersham has been filled in, though Beeston, even if a bit one-sided, is an example on a less impressive scale.

Ickwell is also interesting in being one of the two sites in the County where the ancient fertility rites to celebrate the return of spring are still practised, albeit somewhat self-consciously. Selection as Queen of the May in this cynical age is probably not of the same significance to the average village maiden as when it attempted to recapture rural pleasure after the bleak Cromwellian interlude. We are still burdened in many ways with the Puritan legacy so we should probably be glad to be reminded that one aspect of the Restoration was a partial return to the simple pleasures of a life related to the rhythms of nature and the cycle of the year. At least a pause for a little amusement in an otherwise hard life was not any longer assumed to be frivolous.

As landscape the Green hangs together very well though in the name of infilling there have been some odd perpetrations of the early days of 'neo vernacular', particularly one elephantine job in white painted brickwork and thatch which is too shallow. The whole thing is an affront and out of scale. There has been some efficient and sensitive restoration, and more is needed on the west side where some lovely cottage ranges are quietly mouldering. We can be thankful and proud however that conservation and careful management has been so successful overall.

Spring 1984

KEMPSTON – Church End

Only the *King William* and a few nearby buildings remind one that the main part of Kempston was once a village. The price for urban expansion seems likely to be absorption into the Borough of Bedford although this will obviously continue to be resisted. Rural Kempston is a scattering of 'Ends', and Church End a precarious survival which miraculously did not attract a row or two of villas and the odd 'semi' in the days before planning control. As a prelude to the delightful riverside scenery opposite Biddenham it will probably survive for another decade. The next could see the start of Bedford city and Kempston to Bromham *Swan* an urban strip. It is one of the mysteries of the proliferation of planning proposals in the last few years that they are so often suggested for the most unlikely parts of any region with which one is familiar. Of all the points of the compass, the west, hilly and cut by the river and its flood plains, is surely the obvious one to avoid.

The road to the church recently marred by a large tangle of electrical equipment narrows to the right to open into a delightful triangular 'place' bounded by a range of 18th-century cottages, and a neat red brick Gothic school. Everything is held together by low stone walls and the arched passage through the cottages to the churchyard is charming and unexpected. The scale of the new building adjoining the school is perhaps a little aggressive but it will probably blend in, with time and some judicious planting. One hears of another building site to the south of the school. This should be enough, otherwise the whole distant prospect of this very satisfactory corner will be altered for the worse, a fact which the planners of the 70s would do well to consider.

Summer 1967

Kempston Church End
March 15th 190?
Bernard Bhutt.

KENSWORTH – Church of St. Mary

Social organisation in the years following the Norman Conquest, both of village and countryside, is difficult to comprehend at this distance of time, but the building programme of castle and churches is a lasting testimony. It is at its most eloquent in the small country churches where detail has not been entirely lost by rebuilding. One thinks sadly of the early colonisation of the Cotswold valleys, where with stone so readily available, 19th-century restoration of many a small Norman fabric has been barbaric.

Here at Kensworth, in one of our loveliest Chiltern plateau valleys, St. Mary's is still basically a two cell Norman chapel and probably 'turn of the century', certainly not much later than 1120. The south door is fine and primitive, foxes and cranes carved on capitals, and saltire crosses all around the arch. The original west doorway now leads into the tower, and the carving of the chancel arch also indicates a very early date.

The setting is one of the best in the County on a loop road below the Lynch where a succession of fine houses and farms culminates in a widening to form a small green, with tall trees as a frame to the church on the side of the valley. Nothing could be better than this; even the approach is perfect, a typical sunken way, more characteristic of Hertfordshire, and buildings like Lynch House, for example, are of high architectural quality. This is one area where neither alteration nor infilling should be allowed. All the buildings of whatever merit succeed one another with appropriate gaps and fine stands of trees, and only the jagged profile of suburban ribbon development on the southern ridge is a reminder of our own dreadful 'wen' a mile or two away.

Spring 1979

St Marys Church Kensworth
From West. Dec 1975

KEYSOE – Church of St. Mary

Caissot, the Norman French now thinly disguised by modern spelling, is more accurately pronounced in local dialect than in modern use and is echoed again in old French on the church font asking all '*qui par ici passerz*' to pray for the soul of Warel. One realises that few villages in our area carry such reminders of the Conquest either directly by name or by association. French influence at Court, and in government, persisted well into the 14th century, but this countryside must always have been strongly Anglo-Saxon, particularly here where the real racial mix occurred, and where the later Danish settlement ensured generations of 'free' villages, uninfluenced by fashionable squire or clergy.

With a fine eye for a site, the builders of St. Mary's placed their church to dominate a countryside now largely denuded of its former woodland. Park Wood to the north, for example, habitat of one of our rarest butterflies, is a fragment of its former size, as testified by the earliest Ordnance Survey. It is likely, however, that from the south the open fields have something of their appearance when the church was new; but then, of course, an earlier village would have crowned the ridge as well. Only later with the Enclosures did the main Kimbolton-Bedford road become an attraction and the settlement grew up in the long thin 'waste' strips bordering the road. Keysoe Row was the main colonisation of what till then had probably been common land.

Thus the church is in some isolation, and in spite of one of the most beautiful kept churchyards in the County, shows clearly the problems of maintenance that fall on a scattered and by no means wealthy parish. The north aisle is only just stable, but at least lack of restoration has preserved externally a rare feature, a lot of the original plaster. The interior is barbarically scraped and cries for replastering.

Tower and spire are justly famous, as in the marvellous record of the fall of Will Dickins in April 1718 crying out 'Wot's the matter' on the way down and, save for breaking a leg, surviving his sudden descent from the spire.

All the main structure of the steeple is in fine ashlar, with some extremely sophisticated detail, particularly the belfry lights which are put together with a geometrical precision that compels admiration.

Late Gothic in England brought the composition of tower and spire to a peak of perfection. Where, for instance, is there the equivalent, even in the Low Countries of Louth steeple or in comparable villages on the continent, of designs as accomplished as this at Keysoe?

Winter 1978

Keysoe Church October 1978
Bernard West. P.C.A.

LANGFORD

For a moment, particularly with children coming out of school, one has a glimpse of the urbane Langford that might have been. Looking south-east, Church Cottage (surely grand enough to be Church House) is seen over an animated foreground, and one could imagine the wide street lined with such fine 18th-century facades with the occasional earlier structure gable end on to it as in the foreground. To be fair, modern development has given the area around the church more scale and cohesion that it had twenty years ago, particularly a nice range in the north, where black feather-edge boarded links at first floor level create a sense of enclosure just where most effective. The trees are fine, and the scrappy bleakness of Arlesey and Stotfold is avoided so there is a lot for which to be thankful.

St. Andrew, to Pevsner 'an uncommonly uniform Dec church', is just about perfect. Well maintained inside and out, it has external texture of the warmth one often sees in South Cambridgeshire, cobbles or boulder clay erratics, sandstone, limestone and flint, with beautiful roofs of old peg tiles, and of course the jolly south porch tower. Inside all decent whitewash, just about perfect does indeed sum it up, and how often can one actually say that with conviction?

The window tracery which is carefully and very sensitively restored, considering much of it was originally Totternhoe stone, is varied and in two cases displays the use of spherical triangles, a very subtle feature to be found in the east windows of St. Peter's, Bedford, and All Saints', Ravensden, only here they are triple cusped. A small pity is that the chancel is late 15th century, where one would have welcomed a sort of culmination of the earlier style like we have at Wymington in the north of the County.

All the kerbed memorials – of black and white marble, some filled regrettably with the dreadful green chippings like inflated bath-salts, that have got caught up like a flotilla in slack water – don't help an otherwise perfect churchyard. They all seem stranded in lines against the south churchyard wall. Indeed here it becomes a cemetery and not a churchyard at the one point where a soft and gentle foreground is most needed. At least the other side of the path is fine open space under the trees.

Autumn 1984

LEAGRAVE

I was first taken by John Dony to sample the botanical delights of Leagrave marsh just at the end of the Second World War. It was already a suburb then of course, and as my aunts kept a confectioners' shop in nearby Limbury where I often stayed in the school holidays, I was able to explore the area – the mysterious Wauluds Bank, for example, and the marsh. Here I caught minnows and tadpoles; the landscape then seemed much more remote and unspoiled in spite of the proximity of the railway.

I am often accused of a jaundiced view in the Sketch-book, but I have known this country intimately for forty years, and the expansion of Luton and Dunstable has been for me an unhappy process. An exploration of the Marsh Farm development reveals much charm and careful design, and of course tree planting is embryonic but, all in all, the ambience is forbidding, with a looming water tower like some sinister sentinel. Seen across the one piece of the common which achieves real scale the flats have some grandeur, and must have magnificent westward views, and of course an estate under one design control holds together better than the overspill mish-mash of Houghton Regis for all the excellence of some individual designs. It is the fact that one remembers a rural situation held static by the circumstances of war, which did at least halt the sprawl of the 1930s, the years when Biscot to Limbury ceased to be country. The fact that this corner of Leagrave has survived at least superficially is a lot for which to be thankful.

Here are some of the finest beeches in the County, a species threatened to a lesser extent than was the elm, but seriously at risk. The river is reasonably unpolluted, and the whole beautifully maintained if one ignores the changing-room graffiti which must be a *tour de force*. It is only that one wonders on the next visit how much nearer Luton will be to Streatley, or when it will spill down Barton Cutting.

Autumn 1980

LEIGHTON BUZZARD – Market Cross

We can only guess from the three surviving Eleanor Crosses what the one at Dunstable may have been like. Today there is only a single comparable structure surviving in Bedfordshire, the Market Cross at Leighton. Smaller examples, like the preaching cross at Stevington, are interesting, but simple and unsophisticated compared with the riot of crockets and pinnacles at Leighton Buzzard. Restoration there has been, but it has been carried out with an assurance that leaves few doubts about the authenticity of the details.

It is the treatment of its surroundings that betrays the contemporary lack of appreciation of its setting. This is a marvellous street, with buildings on a scale that does justice to its width; which makes it the more distressing to see the wretched lamp standards that droop their way in mournful procession mauling the skyline or fouling the buildings. In front of the Cross itself is a barbarous clutter of street furniture with a silly little garden at the bottom, recently and rightly condemned in the *Architectural Review*.

In the last few years dreadful threats to Leighton town centre, circulated as rumours, could, as experience elsewhere shows, all too easily be based on fact – demolishing island buildings of great character which perfectly close the view and without which the middle of the town would be a desert; even moving the Cross itself. All this parallel with an enlightened scheme for rehabilitation of facades and fascias by a Civic Trust face-lift.

At last there seems to be a chance that the High Street may become a 'pedestrian precinct' and survive sacrifice to motor traffic – particularly as a road pattern could readily be created behind existing buildings. This would be a real contribution to civilised urban living.

Winter 1964

Leighton Buzzard Market Cross
October 1964. Bernd Bödert.

LEIGHTON LOCK

The creation of Leighton Linslade brought much attractive scenery into the County, not least the lovely towpath walk from the *Globe* to Leighton, on which is situated this the most attractive of many locks of the Grand Union Canal.

The descent to the *Globe*, as unexpected as it is hazardous, brings one to a pub of almost toy-like charm, sensitively extended, and making the very best of its setting; the little 18th-century façade sags towards the canal, and seems propped up by its porch. Lying well below water level one wonders how often canals are subject to flooding – life must be exciting here when this occurs. Towards the swing bridge, the woods below the road to Corbetts Hill Farm slope attractively down to the Ouzel, and around a corner Leighton Lock appears with the distant spire above the trees.

It is extraordinary with what assurance the canal builders handled the landscape in relation to what was a major engineering exercise. The slight gradient here is utilised as something more than just the basis of lock construction. The keeper's house is perfectly sited, and all steps and walls grow naturally out of the need to retain the earth excavated for the overflow tanks. The black and white trim is welcome and familiar, but above all it is the use of brick and natural stone which immediately unites the work with its landscape setting.

Our treatment of a once extensive canal system makes one ponder on the contrast with Western Europe where the narrow boat still has an economic rather than a mainly leisure significance. All the same one is grateful that companies like 'Wyvern Shipping' at Leighton make barge holidays pay, the incomparable landscape of the canals is preserved and a rich rarity of wildlife associated with fresh water brought to areas where it would be otherwise unknown. It just seems amazing that so much canal restoration should have to depend on voluntary labour in a country where freight on the roads is becoming an abomination, and so much bulk could have gone, and in many cases still could go, by water.

Winter 1980

Leighton Lock
Leighton Buzzard
September 30th 1980
Donald Maxwell

LIDLINGTON

What might have been our one good hill village has somehow not quite realised the potential of a really magnificent site. With an imaginative planning policy and sensitive design there could still be development towards the skyline which would give the place the sort of visual lift it so badly needs. The early 19th-century builders of the double-fronted house in the illustration understood the need to punctuate the slope and stand up from it; 'Clayhill' next door, though using the slope to incorporate the garage, nevertheless lies limply on the side of the hill; nor are the infill ranges of standard builders' suburbia worthy of their unusual position.

Round the *Green Man* things are very different – though badly mauled, a grand little group – the pub crouching low and welcoming, a first class piece of recent rehabilitation by Greene King, with a gawky but picturesque group rising above it on the other side of the road. What could have been the original form of the three-gabled red brick range? There are signs of attractive fanlights so it must be late 18th or early 19th century. Before the coming of the brickyards little villages like this must have been poverty stricken, and what has survived from the past, for example another strange apparently late 17th-century house beyond the new Hall, has been so patched up over the years that the stabilisation, in these days of prosperous conversion of any suitable country property, holds in a permanent state the condition it had reached in the lean years. This, however, is vastly preferable to the alternative of forced Tudorisation or worse.

The brickfields have of course brutalised the neighbourhood, one or two uncompromising roads of hard little houses hammering up the hillside are backed by the chimneys, and one is grateful for the Vauxhall 'adventure playground' nearby which rather than detracting from the landscape has enhanced it, and heightened its character. The tree planting is extensive and well advised, and will look magnificent in a few years' time, as that around the maturing lakes of the former pits develops its own vegetation. We may yet see the Bedfordshire Lake District, when Lidlington would be on the map with a vengeance, and one hopes that planning policy will be able to encompass such a possibility. It is one for which forward thinking could well start now.

Autumn 1978

LITTLE BARFORD

Little Barford's separation from its larger namesake is often a matter of comment by visitors to the County, as Roxton and Tempsford lie in between. It is not a village that makes any great impact and unfortunately is always associated with Farmer and Dark's power station, which assumes an importance greater than its architectural merit, sited as it is in a wide flat valley. Indeed, all views to the north-east from the high land at Moggerhanger are closed by this rather unlovely group. Battersea power station spawned some unfortunate progeny which often lacked Scott's handling of mass and detail.

Apart from one good farm and a rather grim thatched range along the street, one is through the village while looking for its centre and there is a strange sense of remoteness in spite of the proximity of the now sprawling suburbs of Eynesbury.

Presumably St. Denis represents the site of a riverside settlement in its present strangely inaccessible situation. Such a location must always have presented a hazard from flooding and the village may have retreated to slightly higher land along the main road. The new house in bungalow Georgian to the south of the church is an acceptable neighbour and its grounds are going to be lovely, though immature at the moment.

The treasure of St. Denis is its very fine Norman south doorway of around 1150. There is a hood mould with dog tooth decoration, characteristic more of the 13th century, so it may be a little later in date. Street has tinkered with the structure without making any particular contribution to the whole. His two-light window in a miniature transept off the chancel is very much out of character but he was of course not a particularly self-effacing architect.

This is again a village which could well support a little expansion, carefully carried out and not in corridor form along the road, but as a close to the east side. This could give the village a centre, which at the moment it sadly lacks.

Winter 1987

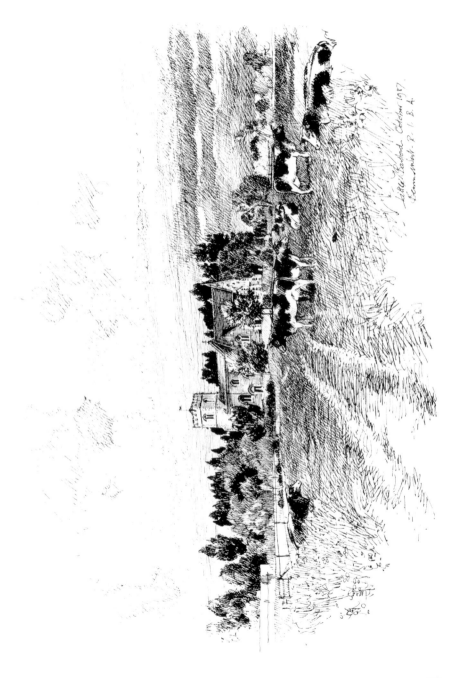

LITTLE STAUGHTON

St. Margaret, isolated from the village, has as commanding a view of the surrounding countryside as Chellington, perhaps even better as it rides the ridge more effectively displaying the mediaeval eye for a site evident at Keysoe, Colmworth and many more inspired churches to the north in the old Huntingdon county. Sites like this may well have been of an old sanctity, like the chalk outliers in the south, but with the development of the spire towards the end of the 13th century it became possible to pinpoint these probably long venerated places much more effectively.

As a composition the church is marred by the heavy roofing in Redland slates, a regrettable development of the concrete tile industry in the early 1950s, which has given a top heavy appearance to many a housing estate and has done so here to the church. The chancel roof is like a large lid with silly bargeboards, more appropriate to some suburban chalet, over the east end. There was a time with the Diocesan scheme for the inspection of churches when such architectural reductions, as they were euphemistically called, were actually recommended. In the name of economy, one supposes, the proper embattled parapet has been removed and what one can only call a 'lid' put on. The same dreadful treatment has ruined the nave of Thurleigh church. It is particularly sad here as the chancel fenestration is a rich and hearty Perpendicular of strong East Anglian character that deserves better.

Little Staughton village can by no stretch of the imagination be called one of our more attractive villages, although there is some excellent modern building in the current 'vernacular' idiom, which is effective and well-mannered. Older work is mostly well conserved with one or two thatched properties surviving, but one half-timbered house has been treated less than sympathetically. In the end, as so often, it is the small gault brick houses of the mid-19th century, often built into the road, which give any sense of enclosure and village character.

Spring 1990

St Margaret, Little Staughton
Desmond West. R.I.B.A. Jan. 90

LOWER GRAVENHURST
– Church of Our Lady

Stripped and silent, save for the cooing of doves and the occasional tick of electric meters, this charming building has entered the first phase of decay. It seems likely that the Diocesan authorities will be urged to declare the building redundant, which would inevitably mean its gradual dissolution and, finally, its demolition. If events take this course it will be a fitting commentary on contemporary values. Lavish and inhuman monuments of the new technocracy stand at no great distance from Chicksands, and to the north are the bright little bungalows of the affluent society; but the old stranded church seems to be without money or friends.

Setting aside spiritual values, it would be less regrettable if the building had no architectural merit; but this is far from being the case. Apart from Dean and Chalgrave there can be few other Bedfordshire churches which so completely retain their architectural integrity as Our Lady of Lower Gravenhurst. It is a simple single-cell building without aisles of mid-14th-century date. The screen and pews are largely original late 15th-century work, well restored and in good condition. There is a fine original king-post roof and a restored Jacobean pulpit and tester. To the left of the altar is a sumptuous wall monument of 1606 to Benjamin Pigott, late Justice of the Peace of the County of Bedford, with intact memorial brasses. The irregular old tile flooring throughout the building is full of character. If all this is to be sacrificed to the demands of expediency then one architect at least will lose faith in the Diocesan Board, whatever arguments are advanced in favour of concentrating funds in those areas where the population is more able to maintain the fabric of their churches.

We must face the facts of the situation. The tide of use has ebbed from Lower Gravenhurst as it has done from the more remote parts of Norfolk, Suffolk and other areas. It is sadly ironical that our ancient buildings are now threatened in inverse proportion to the increasing interest shown in them. Thriving sales of Shell and Pevsner guides, county handbooks, Batsford topographical books and the like can only indicate that this deepening concern with our inheritance has come too late to save it. The society that can now afford cars to visit places of scenic and architectural beauty is employing the chief agent of their destruction.

Autumn 1963

LUTON – Baptistery of Church of St. Mary

The baptistery of Luton Parish Church, work of the late 14th century, is the crowning glory of a building full of treasures. It is a rare, almost unique, example of detailed architectural expression being lavished on the font. There are, of course, the fine wooden font-covers of Norfolk and Suffolk, and corners dedicated to the baptismal rite as at Kimbolton, but here at Luton is a beautifully wrought tabernacle, open to the church – a little building in itself, with a miniature buttressing system that supports a delicate vault within – its rich white stonework seen to fine effect against the shadows of the tower arch.

Luton Church stands in an oasis surrounded by rather drab houses and modern industrial buildings, with great cooling towers, hopelessly out of scale, beyond the east end. It promises little from the outside: one expects the refurbished and brassy interior of a typical town church. Mercifully that is not the case here. The chancel has been rather heavily handled, but in the main the fabric could belong to a country parish of limited means, so graciously have the walls been spared the excesses of the Victorian zeal for restoration. It is in the windows, perhaps, some containing the best modern glass in the County, that a suggestion of the town church is apparent.

Spring 1953

Luton Church
January 1957
Bernard B West

LUTON – Chiltern Green Farm

In spite of the squalor of litter to which the outskirts of Luton are so particularly prone, it is still a surprise to discover the country to the south of the airport. For a few brief miles before one is in Hertfordshire there is a landscape of narrow switchback roads, high hedges and sudden little commons such as this in the illustration, which is still one of considerable charm.

Chiltern Green Farm is in fact sited on the southern boundary of its small green or common, in a small scale landscape which is just about as perfect as it could be: until one looks under the trees. Here once again one is forced to muse on this detritus of affluence, the offcuts of carpet – luxury that someone could not only afford, but was prepared in part to share with the birds and bees as well – a dressing table mirror inexplicably leaning against a tree, the inevitable packaged coal bag filled with garden waste and, of course, car and bicycle fragments which one day will be an indication to the archaeologist of our civilisation, as we find oyster shells and Samian ware of the Romans.

One tries not to become a bore over the litter problem, but we are intriguing as a nation. We are of Teutonic-Scandinavian stock yet naturally as dirty in our habits as in our arrogance we fancy the Latin races to be. Although not obviously solely a British disease, in our essentially small landscape it is all the more offensive.

The farm is a typical piece of late 17th century, half timber, characteristic of all the Chiltern uplands and enriched by that local brick the rich plumminess of which lies at the core of so many south Bedfordshire villages. A lovely place to live in in spite of one's foreground being a dumping ground throughout the year and a parking lot in the summer.

Summer 1973

Chilton Green Farm March 13" 73.
Dennis H. West.

MARSTON MORETAINE – Moat Farm

So many moated sites in the Vale of the Oxford clay have lost their homesteads, many in the last century such as Conquest Bury, some in our own time as at Cardington where one can remember the great gothic fireplaces in a house which should never have been lost. At Marston, in spite of Victorian detailing which is heartless in the fenestration, and with village school chimney stacks, we still have the grand timber-framed Manor of the Snagges. The restoration was the work of the Bedford Estate dating from 1880, and was at least preferable to the wholesale demolition for which the Dukedom was responsible in the last two decades of the 19th century. Any small county seat even remotely likely to threaten the Russell dominance was removed, and we lost many a small country manor house in the process.

The Snagges, whose descendant of boat race fame will be better known than any earlier member of the family, lived here from 1562 to 1712 when Edward Snagge built himself a larger house. Thomas Snagge was M.P. for Bedford for twenty years and died in 1592; he was Speaker of the House of Commons for many years in the reign of the first Elizabeth. His son Thomas was M.P. for Bedford County in 1588, and High Sheriff in 1607 in which year he was one of the first to be knighted by James I.

The house declined in fortune throughout the 18th century, but it has at least survived and apart from the unmoated Meppershall is one of our best examples of its type. Meppershall has better half timber, but here we have the bosky feel of antiquity and a complete moat. The outlook to housing estates is with the village frankly disappointing, echoing to the M1-bound through traffic, and beset by the brick industry. To the south the view across the meadows to the hills would still be recognisable to old Thomas, and the church, but not much else.

Summer 1983

MAULDEN

The dip slope of the Greensand hills, nowhere very clearly defined, is seen at its best on the road from Clophill to Ampthill. The pity is that the glorious view across the valley to the line of the Chilterns is so often obscured by ribbon development of a most unfortunate kind – Osbert Lancaster's 'by-pass variegated' at its most uncouth. Only in the little valley that shelters Maulden village does the scattered development coalesce into a community. Here the mid-Bedfordshire vernacular is seen at its best.

The group illustrated, set around a miniature 'place', represents the best of our mid-county small domestic buildings from the late 17th century to the early 19th century. Adjoining the public house is one coy and inappropriate intrusion – one of those prim little buildings all bright brick and leaded lights for which the *Daily Mail* Ideal Home exhibitions provided the bad influence. The distant thatched range is one of those buildings which are just about perfect; trim with black and white paint and deep thatch, beautifully maintained, it needs the company of some of the best modern building rather than essays in cosy nostalgia.

Only a small proportion of the thatch there must once have been remains at Maulden. The relative frequency with which roof repairs must be carried out has made their cost too great an incubus on the small freeholder. As a result, the ingenuity of local builders has obviously been taxed in covering the formerly thatched 'eyebrows' in tiles; but the final effect is by no means unattractive.

One characteristic of the district deserves final comment – the absence of fencing. In the illustration the foreground is covered with leeks, their blue-green foliage an effective foil to the rich floral display of the neighbouring gardens; across the road rhubarb comes right to the verge. It is, in fact, the southern pattern, every inch of the soil used, as for example in Italy, the absence of hedges or walls saving the pattern from becoming oppressive.

Autumn 1961

MELCHBOURNE

The village has lost nearly everything that once made it of some importance, but still retains an air of dignity as a legacy from greater days. Here was the preceptory of the Knights of St. John of Jerusalem – still standing in Leland's day – around which arose the settlement from which present-day Melchbourne is descended. The subsequent holding of the manor, first by the earls of Bedford and then from 1608 by the St. Johns, was simply a continuation of the estate management. It is interesting to speculate about the refounding of the preceptory in Mary's reign, a brief and no doubt rather desperate interlude amid the social changes of that time.

The cottage ranges of my illustration are late 17th or early 18th century like so much north Bedfordshire village building, but are not on the normal village scale. They are the result rather of the benevolent autocracy that one associates with the estate villages of the west country, such as Milton Abbas. The value of repetition in architecture is here magnificently illustrated. Nothing individually, as a row they are something really out of the ordinary.

St. Mary Magdalene, except for the tower a rebuilding of 1779, is a lovely example of rural classicism; nor is the interior, recently repainted, a disappointment. Contrasting with the simple lines of nave and chancel, the north porch is a mystery. Surely it is late Jacobean work re-erected? If so, its origins are obscure. The detail certainly has no connection with the main body of the church.

Spring 1960

Melchbourne February 4th 1960
Bernard B West.

MEPPERSHALL – Chapel Farm

It is surprising, on the exposed and rather bleak upland between Meppershall and Upper Stondon, to discover, alongside a simple late 18th-century brick farmhouse, a little Norman chapel. The reason for this remarkable survival is that the solid construction of the chapel made it readily convertible into a barn. Its first mention in history was 1291 when its dedication was to St. Thomas the Martyr. The main part of the building dates from about 1175, the chancel rebuilt about 1500. Two excellent detailed little windows were inserted about 1320 into the 12th-century masonry. Both are now blocked. The present west front, with a well-built incongruous Victorian two-centred arch, is modern; but was there a rich frontispiece that was removed to give easier entry for carts? If so, the loss is great. But the survival of the north door is something to be thankful for. It is a typical creation of the period, vigorous, slightly crude, but its moulding already foreshadowing the richness and freedom that was to develop in the following century. Once forming part of the Grange, on the site of which the present farmhouse stands, the chapel has been maintained in excellent condition by the farmer. Internally, good straightforward rendering against damp and other simple repairs indicate a regard for the building as something more than mere storage space. It was no accident in English mediaeval building that so many churches look like barns and so many barns have the dignity of churches, for there was once a closer relationship between church and land. This little building could have had a worse fate to be converted from one use to the other.

Spring 1961

Meppershall, Chapel Farm, &
detail of north door of chapel.
Bernard B West. 1961.

MILLBROOK

High above the modern village, on an obviously pagan site surrounded by the tattered remnants of once fine elms, is a church which plays no visual part in the village in its sunken way below. The mill brook is hard to visualise as adequate for the purpose today and the familiar Bedford Estate housing conjures up no impression of what must once have been a ribbon of cottages and homesteads scattered along the valley. The last survivor of this older identity, built direct onto the road has only recently gone, to be replaced by a silly exercise in a 'nouveau Bedford Estate' style, with ill-proportioned diamond panes, and daft dormers. Does one detect here the hand of the Planner or is it some local builder's idea of the vernacular?

St. Michael, now largely Victorian externally, has Butterfield to thank for this slightly hearty quality. He had a go at it in 1857 and 1864, but left the north aisle east window alone, and to be fair, much of the external masonry, including that of the tower which in coursed ironstone is particularly lovely. The only false note is the bull's eye in the west wall; this can't be Butterfield surely – cement render around a blind hole, and half of it dropped away?

The view to the valley is a bit messy, too industrial, only saved by the Vauxhall test track which is remarkably attractive. Directly to the north the view is somewhat harsh. One need not again explore the arguments for the future of this beleaguered landscape, yet it is reasonable to ponder on a gentler past; the landscape of Page Turner and Fisher, and even the nearly forgotten Sylvester Stannard. The promised land of full rehabilitation is perhaps not for this generation, although it is still our responsibility, or rather that of the Brick Company to keep faith with a more attractive future.

Autumn 1979

MILTON BRYAN

The sad contrast between the *Red Lion* and the Old Post Office is that although the latter is still very much on the sightseer's list, it is the former which is now both alive and picturesque, beautifully maintained and with an exuberance of floral decoration. Nothing plastic in sight, but real hanging baskets, and at the rear a courtyard for dining outside, which is a delight. The Old Post Office has one wing which is derelict, the thin edge of a very dangerous wedge in a timber-framed building and, although the thatch is reasonably sound, the structure is desperately in need of treatment for rising damp, and its social function has long since ceased.

Surprisingly, both buildings are timber-framed, the pub with brick noggin which shows at the rear. It is likely that the brick facing dates from the early 17th century, and the original diaper patterning achieved with glazed headers is still partly evident. The fenestration and general *cottage ornee* character appears to derive from alterations in the 19th century. All is very pretty inside, particularly the dining room, but there is a touch of brewers' Tudor in the bar which strikes a note of discord.

The real Tudor opposite displays some slightly suspect details, but if it is correct that this was once a coaching inn then the open ground floor area at the east end could have been an entrance to stables behind. Today, its supports and brackets have a suspiciously Victorian air while the superstructure seems genuine and, of course, the porches are conspicuously 19th century. It seems that the market value of the whole range, even direct onto the road frontage, could be considerable, and the necessary expenditure for repairs would be daunting. If it is restored one hopes it will be more sensitively than nearby where a former barn has now more the character of one of those Tudor bars the brewers export to the beer drinking areas of northern France or the U.S.A., shiny, smart and deeply suspect.

Winter 1981

MILTON ERNEST

There has been one event or perhaps non-event above all others during the last twenty-five years which could have meant the end of Bedfordshire as recorded in these pages, and this is the scene of what would have been one of the main areas of devastation. As a village centre that at Milton Ernest around its sloping green falls slightly short of its apparent promise from the main road. One wonders whether the demolition of the Turner almshouses of 1695 was really necessary. Today we would, I think, conserve and add in the style of our own times, but the replacement is a bold and acceptable range. The rest is more a matter of fine trees, to the west seen in the grounds of the hall, and to the east as a marvellous composition around the basically simple fabric of the church. All this could have gone beneath a massive embankment of the ends of runways and the imagination is stretched to visualise what a wreckage this would have been. With hindsight of course one can now see that the whole Roskill enquiry [on a third London airport] was a major waste of time and money and based on a premise which is probably already out of date.

Meanwhile Bedfordshire survives and a village like Milton Ernest typifies the pressures of the second half of the 20th century in our much beleaguered County. A fast 'A' road bisects the village, new housing dominates the centre, old barns decay and the fate of the big house has hung in the balance, its future as a hotel typifying the sort of changes that are the price of survival. And yet there is a lot for which to be thankful: a major threat has gone, the general landscape is magnificent and it only needs just the extra ingredient of imagination to clean up the eyesores and smooth away the rough edges. Shall we have begun to think this way after another twenty-five years? There are, thank heaven, signs that we may, so one continues to hope.

Spring 1972

Milton Ernest.
January. 1972.

MOGGERHANGER PARK

Probably the most unlovely member of the vegetable kingdom, natural or evolved, is the brussels sprout, particularly the brussels sprout in old age. This spring the lovely garden front of Moggerhanger Park was dominated by the plant and an ambition to draw the house from St. John's Road nearly thwarted. Nothing can be made of a foreground of the blowsy and decaying stumps.

The view here adjoins a partial clearance of the spinney which has developed over the years on the site of the old sewage disposal system. It contained several good trees which could have remained, and some survive in the remaining half. Is it too much to hope that everything will not be ruthlessly swept away? Each year along this very attractive road another hedge goes, another spinney is grubbed out; one even fears for the future of Sheerhatch Wood itself.

Moggerhanger Park was designed in 1791 by Soane and redesigned by him in 1805 for Stephen Thornton. This, the garden side of seven bays, has a lovely wooden verandah, with above a shallow pediment on pilaster strips with sunk panels. Though the entrance elevation is more eventful, this east front has the delicate, perhaps slightly papery, quality for which so much of Soane's work is noted, and is by far the more attractive. There is no doubt that the utilitarian buildings of the sanatorium do nothing whatever for the house but obviously one must be thankful that such a rough handling in many ways – bombs at Dulwich, and mindless vandalism at the Bank of England for example – that we can ill afford to lose any more.

Moggerhanger as a hilltop village is getting slightly overbuilt, and it is perhaps a pity that the big central square has not been made available for infilling rather than that development as at present should tend to spill over the edges of the hill. The views from the north-west are the important ones, and from this direction Slater's austere and self confident St. John the Evangelist, with its pyramid roof, should always by allowed to dominate.

Summer 1970

Moggerhanger
April 14' 1970
Bernard B West

NORTHILL – The Grange

In 1968 when the Bedfordshire, Huntingdonshire and Peterborough volume of the *Buildings of England* series was published, the Grange at Northill was described as 'not well kept at the time of writing', a description which most happily is no longer true. The building certainly did have a rough time and certain aspects suggest insensitive repair in the past. Old photographs from the turn of the century show only three windows at first floor level on the front elevation and it is interesting to note that the two on either side of the centre lack heads or relieving arches. The Welsh slate roof on the front is a pity; plain tiles would be so much more in scale. One can assume a fairly early date for the Grange, around 1700 or a little later; the door hood on carved brackets is excellent and typical of the date. The old tall hedge has gone and the railings replaced by the present wall and gate piers. One admires the gates – modern copies, with a delightful overthrow, but the anthemions, or Greek honeysuckle, strike a slightly incongruous note and one wonders if they were planted on as a decorative afterthought. Such a combination could not date from the 18th century, as the Greek revival was a 19th-century phenomenon.

This corner of Northill is delightful, made so by the siting of the church and churchyard. Ironically, the lovely view of the church and pub, looking north-west over the village pond, is lost now with the growth of a fine weeping willow. In 1982 when I last drew it one could still look across the water to the church beyond but the tree has increased enormously in size in fourteen years.

The church, which is heavily restored, is memorable in particular for the marvellous windows of 1664 commissioned by the patron of the church, the Grocers' Company. John Oliver, their designer, was keen on his heraldry, but his thinking was more secular than religious.

Autumn 1997

OAKLEY – The River Ouse

The alternation between deep wide reaches of the river and shallow faster flowing sections is a characteristic of the upper part of the Ouse in Bedfordshire. A typical example is the majestic stretch by Bromham Hall contrasted with a shallow stream at Bromham Bridge.

Even before the Conquest many riverside parishes had a watermill and it must have been as early as this that the first control of the river was attempted. Sometimes a side stream would be utilised, less work being involved than in restraining the main waters. As time went on and overall control of the river was the aim, major construction was involved, frequently, as here at Oakley, in association with the landscaping of an estate. Below each mill, dam, sluice or barrage, scour conditions were inevitable, particularly in flood, and at Oakley from the sluice to the bridge, bed-rock and clean gravel tends to replace the usual Ouse mud. It is difficult to visualise the original condition of the valley from Turvey to Kempston, but it is certain that the really magnificent reaches such as this from Oakley to Stevington, would not have existed, not in Bromham before the construction of the barrage. The wide deep reaches belong to the Ouse in middle age, as at Hemingford Grey, but thanks to human activity we can enjoy comparable scenery in a section of the valley where it would not naturally exist.

From the viewpoint on the sluice gates at Oakley the river takes three courses, to the left over a weir, through the sluice, and to the right to the overspill which represents the site of the mill wheel. It is here that the fantastic flood level of the 19th century is recorded. There must have been chaos in this valley then, and this one flood could go some way to explain the disappearance of riverside Oakley. In fact apart from College Farm, only one house, obviously part of a once longer range survives of what was a village street extending to the mill and bridge. Some of this may have gone to suit the landscaping of the park, but the 'Bailiff of the Fens' operating here somewhat prematurely must have been a factor. One hopes that the 1947 floods were the last manifestation of this tendency and that we are now in control, but the Ouse in spate still gives the impression of resentment against the various restraints that bar its course.

Autumn 1965

Oakley. July 1965.
Bernard B West.

ODELL – Church of All Saints

The combination of church and castle at Odell, both on elevated sites, is unique in north Bedfordshire, and with both enriched by magnificent trees affords the artist a wide choice of viewpoints.

In *Ouse's Silent Tide* Farrar was reminded of the Loire when navigating the Odell reach, and the mistletoe in the tall trees which evokes to much of this French atmosphere is still there. To an architect committed to the 20th century the rebuilding of the castle must always seem a lost opportunity; one would so much have appreciated seeing it carried out in contemporary forms, even if in indigenous materials. Nevertheless the combination of outbuildings retained from the past together with the new work is undeniably imposing, particularly from the river, and a site long derelict is alive again. One must also concede that the result is architecturally foursquare and massive even if pastiche, and has none of the jejune quality of the mill which was injudiciously tinkered into a residence some years ago.

The church is of course magnificent even by Northamptonshire standards on the patterns of which parts of it are undeniably modelled. The tower in particular can be recognised as belonging to the Aldwinkle, Titchmarsh type though more crude in detail, and the use of ironstone in the parapet may well point not only to a use of a Nene Valley stone but also the employment of masons from that area. Inside one must lament the mediaeval stained glass if only because enough survives in the south aisle east window by which to measure the worth of what has gone. The group of seraphims in the upper lights have just that combination of sophistication and naivety which makes the closing years of the 15th century so interesting today. A time when spirituality was giving place to a new-found worldliness is not entirely beyond our contemporary comprehension.

Winter 1965

Odell, October 14 1965,
Bernard BW est.

OLD WARDEN

The ties and associations of place are powerful constituents of one's memory of childhood and adolescence. For me Old Warden, within a few yards of this viewpoint, is forever associated with my first experience of a motoring accident. In 1935 my father and I were hit broadside – I wasn't of course driving – by another zealot emerging at speed, and without warning, from the little lane behind my viewpoint. In the ensuing interval of organising arrangements for a lift home, I was left to appreciate, for the first time, the charm of my surroundings.

As the years have passed I have been through the phase of rejection, when *cottage ornee* was a dirty word and one fell in love with what then appeared to be the real thing – the half timber and pargetting of High Suffolk, the integrity of the Cotswolds. One saw this bit of East Bedfordshire as a Victorian stage set, all a bit Birkett Fosterish. Only in recent years has one begun to appreciate the charm of this little oasis between the A1 and the brickfields. One has also begun to understand the general neurosis of the Planners when some years ago they were faced with the Estate, seeking to capitalise on its possessions and carry out some limited infilling. All history now, of course, and the results totally acceptable, but this is not to undervalue the achievement.

My associations intensified when we were excavating the Warden Abbey site in the early 1960s. The *Hare and Hounds* became a sort of upmarket site hut, with fascinating evening conversations after a day's strenuous archaeology. The village centre is a perfect progression of buildings and manicured nature. Clutton at the school, neo-Tudor at the village hall, exquisite late-Georgian with trellis at the vicarage and, above all, the eyebrowed cottage brought to a work of art. The village shop with cupola is a perfect centrepiece. To the west a remarkably formalised elevation, epitomising in its simple way the English love of a rectilinear design combined with the high ground to the south and thick hedges to the north; all is delightful and quite unspoiled.

Spring 1994

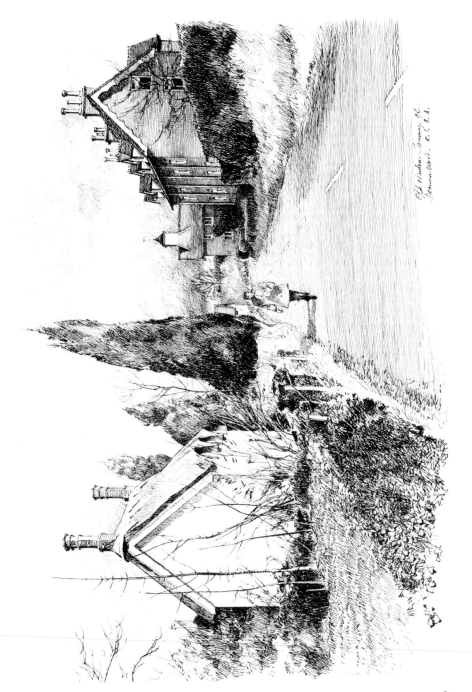

Old Warden, January 96.
Thomas Work. R.I.B.A.

OLD WARDEN
– Interior of Church of St. Leonard

The culminating fantasy in a fantastic village is surely the interior of Old Warden church. An unpretentious, almost drab exterior conceals a bizarre internal richness which is a memorial of the curious aesthetic standards of the mid-19th century. The Victoria County History of 1912, too near 1840 and this monument to Victorian acquisitiveness for a balanced appreciation, considered that it could 'only be called oppressive'. It takes a century or so for a period to return to favour, but the present nostalgia for Victoriana looks perhaps more in envy than in detachment at the self-assurance that could collect and assemble such incompatibilities as these fittings.

According to the authorities, the woodwork is of Italian, English and Flemish origin; but do not the gigantic niches on each side of the altar owe their origin to the austere, sinewy, gothic tradition of southern Germany? Their contrast with the surrounding sensuous Renaissance detail is acute. As in an antique shop, one ponders more on the origin of the things than on their value, on the variant cultures that produced them, on the skill that went into their elaboration, and on the effect their removal had upon the buildings for which they were originally designed. What could possibly be the history of that fantastic snake which undulates along the front of a pew? Is some richly carved Flemish interior now bereft of one of the main characters in its representation of the Fall? In this one small building is a wide diversity of provenance, period and association, but it is unlikely that many of its elements could now be traced to their source.

Sir Samuel Ongley rises above this restless sea of woodwork in Augustan dignity – one of the County's finest 18th-century funerary monuments, beautiful, balanced, finely detailed, and fortunately minus the incongruity of full bottomed wig with toga popular in the 1720s. The epitaph is fulsome but rings true, and the cherubs are delightful.

Summer 1958

Old Warden Church 1958.
Bernard Bewett.

PAVENHAM – Church of St. Peter

The rich woodwork to be seen in Pavenham church is mostly Jacobean, although some is older. Thomas Abbott Green of Pavenham Bury was responsible for the self-imposed task of beautifying this fine if small scale building, and there is no doubt that he succeeded admirably. Much ingenuity has been employed in fitting together what are often diverse fragments, but here and there the joinery is not too satisfactory. The woodwork should not be mistaken for local carpentry. It is an assemblage of pieces of several periods and from several countries; some is Flemish. The subject of my sketch is the pulpit, which is made up of various panels. What appear to be Jacobean overmantel figures mask the corners. They are a good example of the partial digestion of details from the textbooks of Renaissance design which found their way into this country at the end of Elizabeth's reign – vigorous but naïve interpretations of the caryatid figure, the body of which (in a building) acts as a column, with the capital forming a rather unbecoming hat. It was the Greeks who invented this attractive but disconcerting art form. Other good details in Pavenham church are of native craftsmanship – the fine 14th-century canopy work in the north aisle and south chapel, for example. But above all it is the gradual ascent from the nave to the high altar necessitated by the site – so right for a church – which gives especial dignity and significance to the east end.

Spring 1951

Bernard West.
Pavenham January 1951.

PEGSDON

Very rarely does the Bedfordshire landscape assume qualities of breadth or grandeur. Here and there on the Ouse perhaps, or in Woburn Park, but the Chiltern foothills are another matter. The main escarpment to the west of Barton has its highlights, the Clappers at Sharpenhoe or Dunstable's Five Knolls, but the foregrounds are too often mutilated by quarrying, pylons or disfiguring and mean foothill suburbs.

Eastwards there is a lack of high drama but instead a fine scale and modelling, supported by mature stands of timber, and with a foreground intensively farmed but wholly rural. The Pegsdon salient, a piece of the County which projects deeply into Hertfordshire has real nobility which is enhanced by the fine approach from Shillington. This gains much from the regular planting of poplars which give the approach to the hills a very French quality reminiscent of some of the chalk country of the Pas de Calais.

Nearby lies Bedfordshire's only national Nature Reserve at Pegsdon Common Farm, the famous site of Knocking Hoe, long renowned for its pasque flowers and rare orchids. This lies to the north of a characteristic dry valley and is not dramatic as landscape but it is a place of pilgrimage for those with eyes for its less obvious beauties.

Autumn 1971

PERTENHALL – Church of St. Peter

Of all the churches in our County, Pertenhall perhaps retains more of the fittings and architectural incongruities of the late 18th century than any other. Most interesting is the late Georgian chancel extension, where the misguided zeal of some parochial council has produced an extraordinary essay in 'Churchwarden Gothic', with window tracery that would make a mediaeval mason flinch. There are high box pews and a fine, though sadly mauled, chancel screen which in its day may, like that at Felmersham, have had a vaulted front. A charming set of angels, taking the place of crockets, still surrounds the central arch. Parochial poverty has fortunately preserved the interior from the pitch pine and bright encaustic tiles beloved of later 'restorers'.

The early 15th-century broach spire belongs to the big group which spreads from Northamptonshire over our northern boundary and eastwards to the Fens. Old weather-worn tombstones, happily uninvaded by glaring Italian marble, lurch in the tousled churchyard grass.

Nearby stands the fine Georgian rectory, severe but imposing, its façade looking out over the park-like grounds. Fisher sketched the ancient manor house beside the church but restoration and a thick encumbrance of ivy have hidden some of its glory.

Winter 1947

PODINGTON

The attraction of Podington remains undiminished by perhaps the most insensitive tangle of overhead wires and cables to be seen anywhere in the County. Of our three 'Nene Valley' villages this is the most perfect: Wymington can be written off as a suburb of Rushden, and Farndish lacks the architectural richness. Here the High Street is a parade of excellent stone detailing and well-maintained thatch. The most remarkable range, of the 17th century, is based on an extended triumphal arch design centred on a footpath, the outer arches, in dressed ironstone, are blind and on one side sadly cut by a later window. A thatched range has had a gable of little stepped obelisks, only the terminal surviving. It would be a really worthwhile exercise to replace the others.

The 18th-century range in the illustration carries the initials *R.O. 1778*, obviously the Richard Orlebar of the time, and has suffered on the High Street elevation from the addition of a hideous Victorian bay. The pediment behind is deformed by the deflection of an obviously inadequate arch or beam to the new opening. However, the south elevation with its ironstone quoins and string in fine ashlar is perfect, one only regrets the loss of the original stacks, which would have carried the traditional entablature of fine mouldings against the sky, rather than the present competent but less subtle brickwork.

St. Mary the Virgin, an essential part of the High Street, is full of character and beautifully maintained, decent plaster and whitewashed walls internally, and outside a proper country churchyard, neither prettified nor mown and cleared to destruction.

Of course the church is dominated by Orlebar memorials, including a fine range of hatchments and one or two nice examples of funerary art, but in the churchyard there is room for historical conjecture. Here are three Swithland slate headstones from Leicestershire, about as far south as one is likely to find them. One is to John Goosey of 1855, and two commemorate the Smiths, husband and wife, in isolation at the west end of the churchyard. She was buried in 1839, John in 1841, but it is her marvellous Old Testament name of Kerenhappuch which compels attention. One wonders what her surname was before it was Smith, and why they are buried away from the rest; perhaps because of a severe life-style based on some literal interpretation of the gospel.

Southwards at Hornbeam Close the village has had the good fortune to have attracted a small estate as fine as anything in the County. The walling to the road continues the piebald limestone/ironstone tradition, and the houses are restrained and dignified. One remembers seeing this at the design stage and it is rewarding to find the mature reality every bit as attractive as were the drawings.

In the end, however, the abiding beauty of Podington is in its outbuildings, side streets and alleyways. One gets glimpses of large barns which could be in a Fisher engraving, intimate stone-walled gardens, snug cottages set back between high walls, and sudden changes in level. If only the Post Office and others could re-route a few of the wires, this could be one of our best villages.

Spring 1981

POTTON – The Square

Not so long ago this view would not have existed – a point on the credit side when the old Shambles was removed. But the fact that one of the most perfect town squares in Bedfordshire can now be fully comprehended must be set against the memory of the fresh revelation that each side gave as one walked around the old centre block. Now that the important element of surprise has gone it is fortunate that the architectural quality of the square can stand the exposure. Only to the north-east, where the yard of the *Rose and Crown* melts away to Housden's garage, does the sense of enclosure fail, much as it does by the town bridge in Bedford.

The old Shambles was treated shamefully, and after the arcade had been wantonly demolished, on the usual pretexts of public safety, the gaunt remainder was not an edifying spectacle; but it might have been practicable to remodel the central block as it stood, adding new wings. The old design was provincial and in character with the town, whereas the replacement is a little 'Williamsburg' and self-conscious, though admirably detailed. It is the treatment of the ground that fails to tie the square together. The various grass plots and little trees are not urban, in the way that bollards, paving and cobbles would have been, and the off-centre timber bus shelter is disastrous.

The illustration shows part of the south side of the square, the most perfect grouping in Potton, a lovely mixture of formality and informality. Above are ranges of formal windows; below, all kinds of door cases, bow windows, Victorian and modern shop fronts, are jumbled together unselfconsciously. No need here for 'face-lifting'. It is clear that the place is alive, used and properly appreciated.

Spring 1965

Market Square, Potton, Beds.
Bernard Pearce, February 1965.

PULLOXHILL

From Flitton the approach is an ascent to a hill village, austere and open enough to remind one forcibly of northern England. To a large extent the promise is fulfilled. There remain survivors of a robust local tradition of simple building, some houses gaining dramatic settings from the hilly nature of their sites. Inevitably the proximity of Luton and the suburban squalor of Barton have infected the village, but the miserable hen run in front of the *Chequers* has given place to competent development – a small estate whose houses present their gable ends to the main road, adding, with the variation in roof treatment, considerable interest to the general pattern. The two trees in the centre of the illustration form an important element in the street; it is gratifying that they have been retained.

The Grange, which adjoins the new estate, is a good 18th-century brick building with a fine door-head. The *Chequers*, smart in black and white paint, is a credit to Flowers. Further west is the half-timbered Rectory Farm, with thatched cottages beyond. So within 200 yards there are excellent examples of most of the possible local building patterns. Only with the rearing silhouette of an uncouth water tower on the western edge of the parish is there a total loss of scale. Why it was sited to loom gigantically over the village, rather than at a distance where it would have appeared reduced, seems inexplicable.

Two telephone distribution poles call for comment. During the building of the estate the line had been put underground, but immediately afterwards a pole arrived opposite the pub, to make nonsense of the care taken in preserving the trees already mentioned. The other pole, just off the right-hand side of my illustration, has been placed in the one really dignified part of the village, an act of utter insensitivity.

Summer 1962

RENHOLD

The tower of All Saints', Renhold, has a value out of all proportion to its size. Apart from Ravensden church tower, which is obscured from the valley by the bluff of Cleat Hill, it is the only part of any church which holds the eye above the flood plain of the Ouse to the east of Bedford. Barford lies too low, and Colmworth too far back. The setting is ideal, backed by woods, a prelude to the once remote hinterland of North Bedfordshire and with the trees of Howbury Hall, the last piece of landscape of any character until one reaches that delectable four miles from Huntingdon to St. Ives.

Around the church the grouping of houses is perfect, just the right amount of enclosure and surprise. If only it were economical to give back to the big barns the texture they so badly need. Repair of the feather-edged boarding and peg or pantiles to the roofs in the local orange reds, and straw yellow for the pantiles, would make this hilltop perfect. One knows only too well, however, how uneconomical such an outlay would be, though nowhere would it bring more benefit. The various Ends of Renhold are another matter. Individually, many of the cottages in the process of gentrification have probably been idealised but at least saved; the suburbanisation has, however, been intense, particularly at Salph End. It is the views into the valley, however, where the major development of the last twenty years is most readily comprehended. One is reminded of the famous view south-westwards from Harrow, and how between the wars it turned annually more red than green. Here we have a variant in the dark cladding of the industrial estates, itself a good colour, and a sound case of uniformity in planning control. It is just the scale and general sprawl which is daunting against a still agricultural foreground.

All Saints uses the lovely brown cobbles of the boulder clay, the famous erratics, to good effect. What a marvellous colour they are. Small wonder that for cobble infill to ground work and general landscaping they are so hard to get and so costly; worth it though in contrast to the dreadful blue sea cobbles which are so alien inland. The Becher family tablets are good, particularly that to William of 1694 and altogether the little church is lovely, though invariably locked in these barbarous days.

Autumn 1982

Renhold June 1982

RIDGMONT

Ridgmont approached from Ampthill on the A418 is still set in heavily wooded countryside, in direct contrast to the adjoining largely treeless vale, and it is remarkable how little visual impact the M1 has on the surrounding landscape. That this impression is illusory is soon confirmed if one lingers for any length of time in the village centre and if in particular one attempts to draw on the corner which leads down to Junction 13. The horrific intensity of the traffic at this point is unbelievable; enormous articulated lorries are only just able to negotiate the corner and sketching there I felt actually in danger for the first time in any of the slightly unlikely situations where I have sat to get a good view.

One presumes this is traffic from the A1 coming through Shefford, Clophill and Ampthill and is justification for some kind of organised A1/M1 link, controversial though the route for this has already been. Life in what was once an attractive and fairly peaceful hilltop village is, in the week anyway, a grinding bedlam of through traffic.

The village itself is still visually unspoiled; set to the south against the background of a great park, this is a typical Bedford Estate village with a Georgian and early 19th-century core, which moved to the main road from its old centre at Segenhoe after the Enclosures. All Saints by Scott is as out of character with the regional vernacular as only the Victorians could achieve, vaguely Nene Valley in design with a French accent. The square headed treatment of the spire lucarnes, so much favoured by Scott, Butterfield and Clutton, would not be inappropriate in Caen or Bayeux but the composition with the village shop and the adjoining magnificent cedar that is made by the spire is memorable, even if one takes one's life in one's hands to record it!

Autumn 1988

Ridgmont June '88.
Bernard Nott R.I.B.A.

RISELEY

The picture shows a typical example of North Bedfordshire domestic work from Riseley's long main street. Its rural charm is marred by a criss-cross of telephone wires and the inevitable poles, necessities of a century which otherwise has touched the village but lightly.

Lath, plaster and tiling is the vernacular, but there is some half-timber, including here and there the much extended remains of small peasants' dwellings which may be of considerable antiquity. Brick and tiling there is in plenty, much of it in pleasantly weathered orange-red, made before the days of the big industry in the Bedford vale. One house – or rather, group of houses, for there are several dwellings under one roof – shows evidence of a very early core, for above brick walls and comparatively modern roof rises a stone chimney which is almost certainly of 15th-century design; this is to be seen nearly opposite the turning to Keysoe in the centre of the village.

The church is a typical North Beds. fabric of considerable dignity, and has a pinnacled 15th-century tower of the Northamptonshire type. It stands back from the main street across the fields. Riseley mill, which stood on the hill to the east of the village overlooking Swineshead to the north and Keysoe, is now a grass-grown litter of gears and broken timbers. It stood until fairly recently a battered hulk upon its lofty site, symbol of old ways and past days.

Summer 1949

Bernard B West. 79.

ROXTON

The lodge to Roxton House, and the park seen from the main road, suggest a possibly pleasant enough village beyond, but a detour in fact discloses one of the most elegant village high streets in the County. Of course, one or two things have gone slightly adrift in the name of infilling, a particularly clumsy new bungalow comes to mind, and here and there the all too familiar rural decay of collapsing barns and failing thatch, but there are so many pleasant things which dominate that the overall impression is a happy one.

The church, set slightly apart, but not aloof, is toy like in scale and beautifully maintained, with an adjoining church school of well chosen brick, and white trim, just right in scale and a foil for the old building. The church for once is whitewash and order inside with a happy absence of scrape and tuck pointing by those who thought Gothic ought to be naïve. A sad thing is the defaced figures of the rood screen panels, sad as iconoclasm always is because of the hate and prejudice in the jabs and cuts across the faces and the artistic loss involved, for these are works of merit.

Completely different again is the famous thatched chapel, *cottage ornee* externally in thatch and tree trunk columns, internally an amazing contrast, austere regency Gothic with delicate shiny joinery and beautiful detailing – the sort of thing one might expect to come upon in a back street of Lyme Regis, Sidmouth or on the Isle of Wight, but unexpected even in the estate villages of east Bedfordshire.

Finally at the end of the High Street, the *Chequers* and its cottage companion at the gates of the House, with equally charming pantiled and thatched houses opposite. The *Chequers* is grandly crude, the windows with vigorously chamfered reveals, below a cornice of really daring vulgarity; the cottage alongside, beautifully restored, is a delicate thing in comparison and gains a lot by the contrast.

Spring 1969

Roxton. January 1969.
Bernard B. West.

SANDY – Landscape

Among the tree-clad hills of the greensand range, within a stone's throw of the railway and walking distance of the town, is some of the County's most attractive scenery. The district has a quality almost mid-European. Probably it is the relationship of trim unfenced fields and dense woodland, with cottages and smallholding settlements dotted here and there in the broad landscape, which reminds us of Bavaria and the Black Forest. The glory of the woods is the Scots Pine which, although not indigenous to this part of the world, now seems to belong inherently to the bracken-covered hills.

The road to Everton runs beside the cottages in my drawing. Although not in themselves of particular architectural merit, the cottages present examples of an almost instinctive regard for pleasing grouping and relation to landscape, an instance of good taste in planning that is nowadays usually wanting. Thoroughly bad siting is shown by a modern house at the head of the valley – a pre-war building by the look of it. Considering its proximity to the town, more building in this valley is almost inevitable. It is to be hoped that it will be influenced by recent trends in good house design which, even if a little stark, are considerate and sympathetic to their environment.

Summer 1954

SHARNBROOK

Hitherto I have failed to record Sharnbrook in these 'Sketchbook' drawings. I remember drawing Tofte Manor many years ago, also Sharnbrook House from the garden, both of which were for the *Bedfordshire Times*, and also I think the High Street to the west of the vicarage, when old cottages stood directly on the pavement edge. That must have been at the end of the war or just after, before Sharnbrook like so many of our villages was expanded out of all recognition.

Somehow one has been seduced by the more obvious delights of Odell and Felmersham, mainly because of the difficulty of reconciling the many fine elements of Sharnbrook into a coherent view. The centre carries a delightful prospect of the church with the post office in the left foreground but it doesn't make a fair composition to do justice to the place, and in spite of many fine buildings there are few points in the High Street that hang attractively together. The village has been urbanised without becoming urbane and in parts it is frankly overbuilt.

St. Peter's has been gradually isolated into the typical Victorian ideal of a church central to its churchyard whereas it was once ringed around with terraces and cottages, particularly down towards the village centre where in the south-eastern corner there were buildings which make a charming picture in old photographs. The much admired axial development to the north is not to everyone's taste in forcing a line onto the spire, but it has a certain cosy charm. It is the housing to the west and north which makes no such concessions, standard estate work, of good quality but it really could be anywhere. There are some good things in the church not least the neo-rococo monument to Hollingworth Magniac which might just deceive, as it is of 1867, not 1667; the family also put up the unbelievable mausoleum in the churchyard and again this is in a pseudo-historical style.

It is the spire, however, which gives St. Peter's its identity and, although the site of the church predates it by hundreds of years, it now forms an example of the perfect situation for a vertical element in the wide valley, as does Harrold to the west. Started in the 14th century and completed in the late 15th, the flying buttresses and pinnacles are a modern restoration, with the latter a bit mean for the scale of the whole steeple.

Spring 1982

SHEFFORD

The central dilemma of drawing in a town, or indeed taking a photograph, is the ubiquitous car. What does one do about them? One solution is to rise early on Sundays to produce an empty street scene, which by the nature of things is far removed from reality. Over the time it takes to draw, delivery lorries can arrive and block the view completely and cars can draw up at one's viewpoint; there is continuous change but little chance of a clear view. One can satisfy the traditionalist by introducing the odd horse but to turn the drawing into an imitation 19th-century print with coaches is carrying romanticism a bit far. For better or worse the car is now an essential component of the urban scene and we are used to picking out the architecture, not only above the shopfronts but above a sea of shining metalwork. Only the pedestrian precinct has recreated the urbane environment of purely buildings and people. I was lucky here in Shefford to find somewhere to park and to draw from the car; still, this is a small town at the end of the 20th century and more prosperous, well-cared for and in better heart than many of similar size.

Shefford studied in detail can be strange. The housing on the churchyard frontage has gone long ago and St. Michael's, nicely offset to the street, now dominates. Around it are buildings not of great merit but at least interesting in their often wayward detailing. St. Francis' Home is now converted but Nicholls' church of 1887 survives to form a stop to some quite eccentric architecture on the south side of the street; the two gables in timber are weird – a bit like Osbert Lancaster's Pont Street Dutch combined with artists' studios. What is the possible date of the building on the right – excellent detailing of the brick with segmental arched windows and an extraordinary doorcase – is it 18th or early 19th century? There is a cornice on a house and shop towards the church which has the most extraordinary corbel table of five or six offsets, and tall Tudor chimneys.

In Northbridge Street the timber-framing of Barclay's Bank is more Professor Richardson than 16th century. I remember his timber gutters back in the 1950s, a somewhat fickle search for authenticity, which lasted one winter before leaking on to pedestrians in the passage of the pavement below the front of the house.

St. Michael's, mainly of sandstone, was rebuilt in 1822 with the exception of the 14th-century tower. This is of minor architectural merit, and its upper stages frankly scrofulous but, as suggested, more important in the street scene than it perhaps deserves. Internally the only element of note is some attractively remodelled roofs by Mallows and Grocock of 1907.

This leaves for comment only the lamp standards which reminded one while drawing of the Professor's 'pregnant penguins'. Only a few days after my visit, however, slim black replacement standards were being erected – 'starving swans' perhaps? – which at least have the merit of being simple and functional.

Summer 1994

SHELTON – Church of St. Mary the Virgin

The survival of the village as a real community preoccupies many writers of planning and sociological studies and much has been, and doubtless will be, written on the commuter versus native theme. People who by virtue of their professions can actually live anywhere, representatives, consultants and retired people, may augment a dormitory population to the gradual exclusion of former residents who tend to move to neighbouring towns. At best the outlines of the village are retained, often excellent restoration work is done, not infrequently on properties where the work is perhaps a quick means of throwing money away. At worst all community life is replaced by suburban detachment and an overall prettifying of architectural detail takes the character of the place away.

Generally one dreads this fate in a county like ours, so near to London, and one could single out villages or parts of them where the process is far advanced, but here and there the 'never had it so good' years have given impetus to an ever-widening search for escape from suburbia. Not so long ago places like Shelton and Dean were in decline, but to come into Shelton now is to realise the positive side of new life being injected into a place. The process has not so far advanced as to have involved the speculator or for that matter the erection of many new houses, but restoration work has been done, old properties brought to life and verges and hedges are neat and trim, which twenty years ago were overgrown.

St. Mary the Virgin, Shelton, also reflects the former isolation and poverty of the village in that there were never funds for restoration in the dangerous years of the end of the last century. Consequently the fabric survived to an age where conservation was preferred to restoration and retains its interior fittings intact.

Fortunately the previous incumbent was dissuaded from a wish to remove the chancel screen to the north side, to facilitate the fashionable central position for the altar. In so small a congregation there cannot be said to be a very serious separation of priest from people.

Winter 1966

Shelton October 1966.
Bernard B West.

SHILLINGTON – Church of All Saints

Along the line of the Chilterns there are one or two church sites similar to Shillington which differ from those of the usual spring line villages in that the churches are isolated on prominent knolls, sometimes linked to the main hill mass as at Ellesborough, or isolated as here or at Edlesborough. The theory has at times been put forward that these were sites of pagan worship in the late Roman and Early Saxon period, and that the early church in its wisdom sought to suppress the old beliefs by using these particular sites. There is plenty of historical precedent for such action but actual archaeological proof is needed and this could reasonably be expected to lie only under the church itself or to be destroyed by grave digging.

Shillington church has a suspiciously smartened air, although there is sufficient remaining of the original wall faces to soften the texture of the building as a whole. The reason for this amount of work on the building in modern times is probably a combination of 19th-century zeal, the exposed position and the fact that it is too long for its hill top site. This could be the reason for the failure of the west tower in the 18th century, and the brutal blocking of the east window in the 15th century. This east window is the one major architectural loss; it was probably an early 14th-century design of some magnificence, and the present one is a poor substitute made even more grim by the hard rebuilding which has been done on adjoining walls where settlement had taken place.

The road to the hill, though a little hard in general effect, has some nice buildings with Flowers' bright repainting of the pub a punctuation in just the right place among the surrounding gault brickwork. It would be rewarding to introduce a little more colour wash into this street and perhaps one day the school will be rebuilt in a way which will do more justice to such a magnificent site than the present fortress-like Victorian edifice.

Summer 1966

Shillington March 1966
Bernard B West.

SILSOE

Surely the most felicitous grouping along any Bedfordshire street is to be seen at Silsoe. So many of our villages have a single corner or aspect that is photographed and sketched time and time again, but lack complete homogeneity. At Clapham, for instance, the grand church tower rises stark across the fields, but the village has become an awful strip of ribbon development; the *Cross Keys* at Totternhoe nestles unspoiled in its lovely lane, but the raw tide of building and quarrying laps close to its tranquillity. At Silsoe, the eye has a continuous variety of facades and gables on which to linger, and the subtle, if fortuitous, curve of the road introduces the necessary element of surprise at just the right points. Although the road is a main route, all is perfection, and, as so rarely nowadays, the village begins and ends well, particularly towards Luton where the last thatched cottage has recently been sympathetically restored. If the Bedford end is a little less satisfying, there is one outstanding modern bungalow of restrained design which is an object lesson in architectural good manners. The new estate being built just beyond is in a slightly barbarous neo-Georgian, a style that should long have been dead but shows no signs of lying down. An opportunity for building in an indigenous but contemporary style has been missed in a vain attempt to 'fit in' by the application of so many yards of pediment and cornice.

Silsoe church is a modern building, but by a sensitive and intelligent mind. How easily we might have had some displaced Nene valley spire or the lovely local sandstone mixed with limestone in a hideous caricature of the stripped walls of Northamptonshire, that Mecca of the Victorian ecclesiologist. Happily, the architect spared us all this and gave his church a simple Bedfordshire silhouette, its tower a typical turret, and built it with the local stone.

The one unexpected architectural feature is Wrest. It would be no great surprise to see beyond the little lodges the great silhouette of Chambord or the *tourelles* of the Chateau d'O. What we have is French enough, and yet how right it seems. Dr Farrar wrote in his *Ouse's Silent Tide* that Odell Castle with its great poplars full of mistletoe made him think he was on the Loire. Wrest is a deliberate evocation of France which even its landscape enhances into something quite alien to Bedfordshire; yet it seems right. Is this through familiarity or is the style just sufficiently anglicised to be at home?

Autumn 1955

SOULDROP

In spite of being in sound of the railway this is a remote village on the edge of a little folded valley which in many ways reminds one of distant Dorset, in particular the approach to Church Farm, steep-banked and intimate.

Generally, the village tends to be an infilling job but there are many stone survivors, mostly with sympathetic fenestration. All Saints' Church is interesting in several ways. It has the earliest spire in the County, of the late 13th century and perfectly formed, of broach pattern. Quite an advance on some contemporary examples in Northamptonshire, such as King's Cliffe or Barnack.

Clutton worked on the church – a complete rebuilding in 1861 – and he rebuilt the school at the same time, very much in the manner of his work at Old Warden school. He vaulted the chancel somewhat incongruously, on a small scale, similar to his work at St. Mary's, Woburn, and the organ chamber and porch. The detail as one expects from Clutton is French. Strange how many 19th-century architects saw the Ile de France as the true home of Gothic. Why they ignored the achievements at Wells as early as 1174 or Bishop Hugh's work at Lincoln ten years later, is hard to understand. At the risk of chauvinism, our Gothic was in many ways more home grown and pure, and shook off its Romanesque past more quickly.

Souldrop's achievement is not to have become a suburb of Rushden, as is so sadly the case with Wymington. Only the dreadful Castaways Club on the A6 is a reminder of the standards of the 'boot and shoe' towns to the north.

Winter 1986

Souldrop Oct. 1st 88
Dennis Web. R.I.B.A.

SOUTHILL – Church of All Saints

Southill church has no place in the magnificent landscape of the neighbouring park, which is essentially a great tree-fringed amphitheatre of water and meadowland created to form a foreground to the House. It lies behind the scenes, a memorial to a society quite alien to the near-paganism of the rich 18th-century landlords. Yet the fortuitous result is that the tower – pale almost ghostly against its backcloth of foliage – makes a very satisfactory composition, and one which would certainly have astonished its builders, so unmediaeval is this epitome of the picturesque. To have, as in my viewpoint, three vertical forms competing with a fourth and dominating it, contradicts all the canons of architecture in landscape, but the scale of the enormous trees is such that the church tower acts as a foil to them rather than they to the tower.

Except for most of the tower, with its wonderful texture of weathered sandstone, limestone and plaster, All Saints has a hard look, slightly mechanical and thin in its details. The interior confirms this impression though there is an austere, almost 'dissenting', dignity about it. All this is due to the restoration of 1814, which came a little too late for 'gothick' romance and a little too early for archaeological accuracy – probably just as well, for a hearty Victorian rebuilding might not have left the tower alone. A barbarous feature is the blocked tower arch which ruins the interior by truncating the nave and darkening the west end already overshadowed by the great tree outside. The church is poor in funerary monuments but is the burial place of a famous man of ill-starred fortune, Admiral John Byng, whose execution on his own quarterdeck in 1757 was a sad commentary on the scapegoat justice of the time.

The countryside and neighbouring village form with the park part of the attractive though artificial 'estate country' of which Old Warden is usually considered the crowning glory. I prefer Southill; it has suffered none of the overbuilding of Ickwell; it retains enough solid 18th-century elements to avoid becoming precious, and competent estate management has prevented the seediness which is regrettably affecting Northill.

Winter 1958

Southill July 1958 Bernard B West.

STAGSDEN

The only acceptable part of Stagsden, where the bedlam of the massive lorries on the A422 is only a distant rumble, is to the north of the church and along the first part of that delightful lane to the Turvey road. The rest of the village which, particularly in the central section, retains most of its character, is hard to enjoy. One clings to the narrow pavements cursing Beeching for the closure of so much of the railways as the juggernauts thunder past. Both the east/west routes in the County, this and the A428, now support traffic to and from the east coast ports on a scale which is eventually likely to ruin Bromham bridge, disembowel Stagsden and even make places with an internal bypass like Turvey miserable with fumes and noise. Perhaps the A1-M1 link will bring relief; one certainly hopes so.

The central feature of the High Street is now Mr Willmott's thatching at Joel Cottage, a *tour de force* with the final adornment of straw sculpture. If there is just a suggestion of Disneyland in the final effect, one overlooks this in the face of consummate craftsmanship. The rest of the street combines 17th- to 19th-century buildings very successfully, with the church magnificently sited at the curve of the road and on a very slight elevation. For a hilltop village, Stagsden begins and ends quite well considering its nearness to Bedford. The most sensitive approach is from the west, where new housing has not harmed the grouping seen externally almost from the County boundary over open country. Only the inevitable elm disease has spoiled the former grandeur of the big overhanging crowns of the trees around the tower of the church. Repeatedly old photographs or one's own drawings are a reminder of what a tragic effect the disease has had on our countryside.

Autumn 1975

STANBRIDGE

A lot of villages within the orbit of London's influence have former village pubs which have become out of town venues for business hospitality or fashionable 'watering holes'. The phenomenon is familiar and to be expected in the Thames Valley but it manifests itself further north, the *Bell* at Aston Clinton being an example. There is nothing to regret in this if the village regular is not excluded, but sadly this is often the case. At the *Five Bells*, Stanbridge, I feel the locals may be a little intimidated but it keeps the character of a village pub, which is the secret of much of its charm.

This is a phenomenon of the Home Counties/southern character of our County and is no way surprising, but Luton and its former country cousin, Dunstable, also impose a massive strain on the rural character of this end of Bedfordshire. At Stanbridge, St. John's church and its surrounding buildings – the farm is somewhat out of my picture – are a fitting termination to the green. The other end is architecturally inadequate as the *Five Bells* lies back, but it is a good open space despite being somewhat hammered by traffic on its northern side.

St. John's is the standard south Bedfordshire/north Hertfordshire compact little church, with a squat tower and staircase turret, here in a particularly happy combination of sandstone and Totternhoe clunch. We are spared the usual cement render strait-jacket as the materials, both sandstone and chalk, must have come from good beds, as the weathering is not as bad as usual.

An odd detail is the change in the level of the string course below the belfry windows on the south face of the tower. One often has the feeling that the mediaeval designers' concept of symmetry (or a complete lack of it) indicates an entirely different approach to architectural principles from what has until recently been the contemporary balanced way of handling architectural elements. Is the post-Modern perversity in using incompatible elements a sort of throw-back, or is one reading too much into the design of a small village church tower?

Autumn 1991

STEPPINGLEY

The centre of the village is very pleasantly composed around a dangerous junction of cross roads with the expansive forecourt to the *French Horn* offering an attractive refuge. In fact this must be one of the most welcoming approaches to a pub in the County and, in general, it lives up to one's expectations. A rather bland 19th-century elevation has been prettified with shutters and diamond pane glazing, doubtless replacing the traditional double hung sashes, but the setting and length of frontage compensate. Internally, there is evidence of an older structure but the original timbers are reduced to a certain insignificance by the applied brewers' Tudor which surround them. A study could well be made of this atavistic pre-occupation with an imaginary 'olde world', as if beer can only be drunk with half timber.

Henry Clutton, ubiquitous in mid-Bedfordshire, has been at work here, in the 1860s, for his patron the 8th Duke of Bedford, a loyal client if ever there was one. The usual wayward detailing is his signature, a traditional 'Home Counties' church is subtly altered in every respect with his excessive chamfering and the strange hood mould stops. As at Souldrop and Woburn the detailing is French, grafted onto familiar English forms.

Also by Clutton, the School Room and School House are in a sort of Tudor caricature, but with the church, make a memorable group which recent infilling has done nothing to destroy. Indeed the Local Authority housing on the corner is ideally related to the centre of the village, though a little institutional in its detailing.

Autumn 1987

STEVINGTON – Windmill

Stevington Windmill, though practically unknown to the average Bedfordian, is one of the finest survivals in the County. Though no longer in use, it is as sound as when it was erected over a hundred and sixty years ago.

The mill is a type known as post construction, common in districts where there is plenty of timber. The base is of local limestone, with big struts built into it to support the structure above. Post-mills are constructed so that the sails can always be faced to the direction of the wind; the whole body of the mill above the base around the central post can be turned with very little trouble as is necessary

The mill existed in the open fields before the enclosure of the village in 1806–7. The field in which it stands is the only one in the parish which still retains the original lines of the first enclosure plan. Before it was ploughed up during the war the old terrace lines of strip cultivation could be seen.

I well remember the afternoon I drew the mill. As my father and I emerged from the shade of the trees at the corner of the field and crossed the stubble in the blazing glory of a mid-August day, blue in the distance lay the Ouse Valley, the only sounds a distant tractor and the monotonous call of a yellowhammer. Many such summers the mill must have seen and now it stands, still slightly straining in the wind, a symbol of a way of life, of an economy that can never return.

Summer 1947

STEVINGTON

The *Sketch-book* began with Stevington Mill in 1947 and was actually a reprint of an illustration from a series called 'Our Heritage', in the *Bedfordshire Times* which ran until I was posted abroad. 'Touchstone', alias Chris Carter, wrote the articles. I wasn't allowed to air my prejudices in those days. As the winter issue of the Magazine carried an article on the mill, I thought it might be appropriate to finish my fifty years by returning to the village centre.

For me there has always been something about Stevington, a particular *genius loci* which has persisted. My associations go back to the days of dear old Canon Sproule who was always very kind and helpful, particularly with a project I did on the village in the 1940s. Later Edward Bennett became the incumbent, a former BMS master who encouraged my interest in botany and natural history generally. Latterly, Geoffrey Cowley, an old colleague and adversary who, 'seeing the light', deserted Planning and became vicar, with a line in rousing sermons.

Probably my longest and fondest memories centre on Meeting Farm, in the days when Ken Prentice's mother and father were alive and later when Ken himself took over. It became a tradition to go fishing the day after Boxing Day, on that lovely stretch of river between the Marsh and Woodcraft Wood. If my father haunts anywhere it must be there, because he loved this part of the valley. Some things are fixed in the memory: Sir Richard Wells sitting on a log late one winter's afternoon, tearfully oblivious of my approach, mourning the loss of yet another son; the way our small fires for baking potatoes died down and the robins would sit above the embers, wings akimbo for a final warm up before dusk; the prospect of the vicarage at Pavenham across the meadows of Westfields; the day a kingfisher sat on my rod. These are the associations of what Teutonic sentimentality calls *Heimatsland*, and for which we studiously avoid having an appropriate equivalent. I have always been glad of this identification with one area in my lifetime with all its associations, and particularly to the *Beds Mag* for the opportunity to indulge my affection for my native County, and to be able to record my evolving appreciation of it.

Finally, to return to Stevington at the end of the 20th century, and reasonably characteristic of the changes of the last fifty years; slightly

gentrified, and more a dormitory now. It still holds together very well.
There are small regrets, the old approach to the centre had a certain drama,
which has gone with road widening and the setting back of the stone wall. I
regretted that the churchyard retaining wall was rather cheaply rebuilt after
collapse in the 1960s but the snowdrops still bloom above it in profusion, and
the strange butterbur jungle below remains. One can in fact still recognise the
place, which is more than can be said for several less fortunate villages, and
long may this character survive.

Spring 1998

STOTFOLD MILL from Astwick

Of the two mills of Stotfold, this one is virtually in Astwick, and has much of that village's character and charm. A direct contrast to the amorphous sprawl of the bigger neighbour. In the past Stotfold and Astwick were separated by a marshy 'no-man's land', the present road link being of post-enclosure date and associated with a major scheme of land drainage.

The structure of the mill, and the millhouse, as it stands today is largely of mid-18th-century date, with a delightful garden flanking the river. What a pity it is that so much pollution still goes on in the Ivel. One will probably be told that the toxic levels are not a danger to health, but at the other Stotfold mill the river smells and here, although to some degrees oxygenated, the waste in the river is recognisable. There have been years recently when this poor little watercourse has been foul by any standards and one realises just how basically uncivilised is any society that treats such natural resources as a sewer. One is not very satisfied either by the way the river authority does its dredging, where the mud, weeds, roots and junk are dumped arbitrarily along the banks without any attempt at spreading or landscaping.

In an area where the hedges have gone and the landscape sacrifices to agriculture have undoubtedly been greater than is warranted by the economic return, a small river, with its willows and footpaths on the banks, is an asset. Squander this asset and it is not readily replaced when and if we ever take to our feet again and forsake the weekend scramble to the coast for the use of the still attractive footpaths and waterways nearer home.

Winter 1970

STREATLEY – The Old Forge

The church and the *Chequers* at Streatley, and the fine 18th-century house next door, ought to compose into a fine group, particularly as the pub is so well sited on a slope up to the churchyard gates. Disappointingly, however, there is no point where these elements combine, a situation similar to Tebworth or Wrestlingworth where there are individual buildings of merit isolated from each other and often obscured by trees or a high fence or hedge. This is a pity as Streatley is something of a survivor when one looks at Houghton Regis, Sundon, or even beleaguered Barton. There is some very good new housing as well, both brickwork colour and detailing are a delight, particularly across the road from the *Chequers*.

However, just to the south there is a charming little group, the Old Forge which has been sensitively converted to a house without altogether losing the character and memory of its former function. The two little round-headed windows, their rubbed brick arches standing out red against the gault brickwork are perfect, as is the porch. Mrs Waters of Stanley Road, who was good enough to bring me coffee and a picnic while I was drawing, can remember horses still tethered there for shoeing as recently as thirty years ago. The way the buildings are tucked into the slope, with an adjoining miniature 'green', maintains a rural aspect in contrast to the modern housing across the road.

One wonders about Streatley; the wide plateau punctuated by Warden and Galley Hills, seems ripe for conquest, with the front line already at Bramingham. Just how far will Luton spread? The Hoo stops it southwards, which doesn't augur well for the opposite direction.

Winter 1993

STUDHAM

Travelling south from Kensworth, one approaches Studham through our one fair sample of true Chiltern country, with many of the characteristics of nearby and more famous Ashridge. One can still recognise the lovely contrast of open common land with the dense woodland of the Chiltern plateau, which reflects the soil cover of clay with flints over the underlying chalk. Apart from the regrettable development of Oldhill Wood, an early Planning blunder, and the ploughing of a lot of the grassland, this is still a very fine landscape. Studham itself doesn't quite live up to its setting, lacking as it does any really sophisticated 18th-century building in the one place where it tightens up nicely into a compact village street. The scattered housing and road frontage development also slightly blur the pattern of early settlement which is likely to have been originally one of 'squatting' around and even on common land, during and after Enclosures. It is still however attractive in its hollow, with the surrounding rising land.

One does wonder though why we need so many signs, lights and what Ian Nairn used to call 'things in fields'. The street lighting is intrusive in the village setting, and there seem to be junction boxes, posts, name plates, everywhere; and of course the 1951 name boards, now sadly somewhat *passé*. It is probably churlish to add that the traffic island planting is also a trifle suburban. One or two semi-mature trees would have been preferable; whitebeam for example would be entirely appropriate.

Away out of sight, and presumably representing the core of the original settlement, at first doubtless a clearing in the woods, St. Mary's church lurks at the end of its still leafy lane. The interior is a surprise after the bland cemented exterior, and contains up to date detailing of 1220 or thereabouts, together with some coarse capitals looking more like 1190 and almost still Norman. Was this an old and a young man working together, as has been suggested, perhaps even father and son?

Winter 1997

SUNDON

Sundon and Streatley with Sharpenhoe are a phenomenon. That they are there at all and recognisable is testimony to the control of sprawl which may be negative planning control, but is undeniably preferable to the chaos which prevails in Leagrave and Limbury and which otherwise would have spilt out across this countryside. Whether what has been saved is true country is of course another matter and one is acutely aware of the proximity of a large urban population, a proportion at least of which is increasingly pressing for rural freedom. Apart from Dunstable Downs and Whipsnade where overcrowding from greater London is now acute, and Warden Hill which is mainly golf there are not many places to go, and this triangle bounded by the A6, the escarpment and the railway, with Bramingham Road the southern boundary, is prairie farming to the very edge of Sundon Park. Visually it loses trees each year, the tangle of wire and pylons dominates and megalopolis looms to the south; it is not country to enjoy any more. The farmer shows his contempt for it by igniting large areas each harvest and the townsman by leaving his old mattresses, prams and motorcycles on the verge. So what is the future of a village like Sundon and its surrounding land?

The escarpment is magnificent but inaccessible, except for the Clappers, even to the extent of still carrying unexploded ammunition in one place, over twenty years since the end of the last war. This is of course just too damn silly, apart from being dangerous, and it is a measure of our national and local lethargy that we put up with it. All this wonderful range of hills should be available. In such a stretch of country something might be done about the inculcation of rural values in an urban population. At the moment while the Local Authority, the speculator, some farmers, and statutory undertakings defile the land, the rubbish dumper sees nothing illogical in leaving the sort of mess which was in the ditch behind me when I drew Sundon Church. A child playing there could have been lacerated, poisoned or disembowelled, and one can well believe Luton Rural RDC when they say that the litter problem is one with which they already cannot cope. It is probably quite illogical to suggest more countryside parks when the mess is beyond the Local Authority already, but there is something in the latest trend of not supplying litter bins at all and suggesting that the visitor should leave only his footprints.

Sundon church has a fine setting if one doesn't look too carefully at broken fences, unkempt land and litter; a uniform mid-14th-century building with the exception of the tower and the chancel it contains one of those unexpected details which delight the antiquary. All the fenestration is good simple country work of about 1330 except the east window to the north aisle which is exquisite and about thirty years out of date. Of fine geometrical tracery it is blandly planted onto the simple jambs and mullions which match the other windows.

Winter 1968

Sundon, October 1968.
Bernard B West.

SUTTON – Packhorse Bridge

The Sutton packhorse bridge suffers like so many rare survivals from being over illustrated and over visited, particularly in a county where only rarely does the landscape and its constituent elements compose into popular conception of the picturesque. For years one found this particular valley a little Birkett Fosterish, but in the expanding desert of east Bedfordshire with its burnt fields and vanishing hedgerows one is now grateful for Sutton Park and the fine trees from Church Farm east to the crossroads. The bridge seen in this context has the charm of rarity which transcends the fact that one has seen it repeatedly in calendar and guide book.

Dating for a structure of this sort is difficult but it is certain that the parapets of the main part of the bridge are original, and in character, have the refinement of the late 14th century, a conclusion which seems supported by the height and sharpness of the arches. In general trim and maintenance the whole thing is delightful, but could one perhaps plead to the County Council for some of their excellent post and rail fencing on the north side – to the right in the illustration. The tumbledown bits and pieces there at the moment make no sort of contribution to the general composition. The ford is delightful and one hopes that no attempt will ever be made to create any kind of bridge, thus destroying the identity of the stream and that of the packhorse bridge in turn. Taken steadily, even in winter, there is no reason why one's brakes should be affected.

Winter 1967

Sutton packhorse bridge
October 1967.
David Birtt.

SUTTON – Church of All Saints

A really rare survival, a truly unrestored church, no signs of the effects of the Camden Society or 19th-century zeal in any form. One enters a perfect interior of 18th-century benches and 17th-century box pews, with a lovely pulpit of 1628 and a sounding board. The basic fabric is also perfect, with elaborate sedilia and piscina, that in the south aisle somewhat smothered by the box pews but this is a small price to pay.

However, it is the monuments which draw the traveller to All Saints and in particular the name of Grinling Gibbons. The series of Burgoyne tombs is magnificent, but it must be admitted at once that the one to Sir Roger of 1679 by Gibbons is the least attractive. The urn on top of a bloated strigillated sarcophagus is far too high up and top heavy and only the garlands at each side are in the familiar style of the master. The memorial to John Burgoyne of 1709 by Gunnis, a reredos somewhat blocking the north aisle east window, is a work of great refinement, seen to disadvantage always *contre-jour*, particularly in the morning, but with some lovely details. The urns in particular are exquisite, as are the weeping *putti* in support at a lower level.

Most visitors will probably enjoy the Jacobean (just) exuberance of the earlier John Burgoyne monument of 1604, with its magnificent effigy in full armour. Based on the early use of the principle of the triumphal arch, with quite scholarly classical details, it is still a *tour de force* of strapwork and obelisks as one would expect of work still within the Elizabethan tradition of *nouveau riche* exuberance.

The exterior of the church is perfect and beautifully maintained and fortunate in grouping with an attractive farm and rectory, Victorian on the east to the ford but half-timbered and sensitively restored to the south. We are lucky with central Sutton; one hopes every effort will be made to ensure its survival.

Summer 1987

Sutton. April 87
Bernard Wat. R.I.B.A.

SWINESHEAD – Church of St. Nicholas

Begun in 1330 and carried through to completion in thirty years with little subsequent alteration, St. Nicholas, Swineshead, may be counted as one of our most valuable architectural possessions. Not only has it much intrinsic merit but, having survived the 19th century unravished, it gives any unusually good impression of the appearance of a small country church at the end of the 16th century soon after the Reformation.

The fabric is extremely interesting – in one part accomplished, in another rural and naïve. The chancel, apparently the earliest part to be built, is full of fine detail assembled and carried out with an assurance that the west tower and spire lacks. Yet the latter composition, which owes so much to the great towers and spires of the Nene valley, and to Keyston in particular, is surely the most appealing and evocative part of the whole church. Was it perhaps erected by a local mason who, recalling the achievements of a few miles away, desired to emulate them in his own village?

The parochial church council has recently completed the lighting of the body of the church, the vicar having arranged for the floodlighting of the chancel; thus modern benefits have been brought to a venerable building in a manner which considerably enhances the beauty of the interior.

Winter 1951

TEBWORTH

Tebworth could do with a little refinement. There is so much that is basically attractive, but where there should be thatch or tiled one faces the inevitable red painted corrugated iron, and in general the potential of the place is not quite realised. One of the most attractive features of this sort of hamlet, and one sees it even in poor beaten about Hockliffe nearby, is the quiet urbanity of the ranges of late 18th- and early 19th-century cottages, as in the illustration. The worrying thing is that it is the middle aged and older one sees in the beautifully tended gardens, so right with their formally clipped hedges and simple brick boundary walls. The younger generation, if they stay, live in the standard semis, forced in if the frontage is adequate, and set back to some so-called but threatening improvement line. This is never what infilling should mean, but it is easier to sell a standard design and of course cheaper to build it. Tebworth has its share of the phenomenon so should treasure the sort of group here because this is the character of the place, not that of the accepted picturesque qualities of one or two thatched and half-timbered survivors, such as the store, attractive though these obviously are.

This whole question of village compactness is fundamental, but while the County Surveyor's Department with its vision splays, set backs and improvement lines is the real planning authority, the sense of community of little places like Tebworth is at risk. The writer remembers the plans for one piece of infilling there which was wonderfully imaginative if unorthodox; what has been built is standard and dull. One knows only too well why.

Autumn 1969

Tebworth, June 69.
Bernard H West.

TEMPSFORD

Except for a few miles on either side of Toplers Hill, the Great North Road from Baldock to Eaton Socon is a ruthless thoroughfare. Tempsford lies astride this artery between north and south. So far it has not paid the penalty which has ruined villages like Stilton; in fact for a place so obviously vulnerable its retention of village character is little short of miraculous. But how long will it be before the advent of a couple of transport cafes, an assortment of filling stations, some concrete lamps and a few hearty posters for petrol, pills and Persil?

St. Peter's church is an extraordinary building which suffered considerable alteration in 1621 at a time when provincial Gothic, except in Warwick and Oxford, was a precarious survival of folk tradition. The repairs to the nave arcades are a good attempt at archaeological accuracy but it is hard to accept the heavy-handed treatment of the 1874 'restoration', which has left the tower a patchwork of materials with typical 19th-century school chapel details, correct enough but mechanical and wiry. The rash of striped walling is probably attributable to a heavy dose of Nene Valley influence which the architect was working out of his system and some of the arbitrary junctions of new and old work are fantastic, particularly in the clerestory. For all this, St. Peter's is a fascinating building, a monument to the fluctuations of taste of three distinct periods.

The fine example of half-timbering of Gannock House is probably late 16th or early 17th century in date, a bizarre contrast in its black and white construction to the Victorian chequer-board walling of the churchyard, itself a legitimate if unusual combination of ironstone and ashlar blocks.

Spring 1959

Tempsford January. Bernard West.

THURLEIGH

This cottage group is characteristic of the excellent condition of most of the north Bedfordshire villages. Re-thatched, bright with new paint and often having undergone structural repairs that are not at once evidenced by external signs, these little structures are good for many more years. One delightful touch here is the abrupt curve on the little outbuilding to the left of the foreground cottage. Was it so built to fit into its site, or just for some personal whim of its builder many years ago?

Thurleigh's chief fame is for its castle mound, which is crowned by a giant walnut tree that can be seen as a sapling in Fisher's illustration made early in the 19th century. It is a far cry from today's prim little settlement around the mound, set in an orderly countryside, to the days of stockades and unreclaimed woodland when the Norman conquerors were subduing the Anglo-Saxons. Part of the Church – the base of the tower, with its notable Adam-and-Eve doorway – must have been built within a few years of the castle, no doubt inside its defences of which even today there are still many traces around the village. Phonologists and strangers should note that the *leigh* in Thurleigh is pronounced *lie*, not *lea*.

Autumn 1953

Thurleigh August 1st Bernard Billett.

TILSWORTH

The chalk downland has always been an attraction to anyone living in the north of the County, principally for its landscape and wildlife. In my cycling days, Totternhoe Knolls was a particular goal. The route always seemed to involve passing through Tilsworth on the way to the hills. I see however in one of my old diaries that on 4 September 1944 I visited All Saints' Church and did drawings of both the exterior and interior; this was also the day that I first discovered the beautiful Adonis Blue butterfly on the Knolls. Tilsworth at the foot of the hills must once have been an open straggle of fairly isolated buildings which would always have lacked a centre of green, like that of neighbouring Stanbridge. The church at the end, with its commanding view of the hills, must always have dominated and is a delightful building worthy of its site. Mainly of sandstone it is a chequerboard of this and Totternhoe stone, but there is also stone from the upper oolitic exposures in Buckinghamshire. It is interesting that these stop just short of Bedfordshire, in fact a little north of Aylesbury, where unexpected stone walling is found in the villages well away from the limestones of the Ouse valley.

The church is locked these days, and one looks back almost nostalgically to the 1940s when we were only concerned with national security. The interior is interesting if not spectacular, for example the way in which the west tower has been built at a later date into what is now only a three bay 13th-century arcade, and the monuments are worth a visit, one being magnificent, a canopy on four slender columns without an effigy. This is of 1582, to Gabriel Fowler. That to Sir Henry Chester of 1666 is not of comparable quality and its kneeling figures verge on the incompetent. A little stained glass survives, and there are some odd statues of soldiers which seem to be 13th century. One wonders if they fitted into a monument or were always free standing. The churchyard gates are of a standard 19th-century pattern, but interesting because of their unusual posts which look exactly like dressed sarsens, the two outer ones having raked flanks, evocative of prehistoric standing stones. Are they actually sarsenstone, or millstone grit? There were occasional patches of sarsens in the Chilterns I believe, but of course nothing to match those of Wiltshire.

The other notable survival in Tilsworth is to be seen at Manor Farm, where the 15th-century gateway with its half-hipped 18th-century roof leads to a rather unsatisfactory display of suburban Tudor. One supposes that a sort of miniature Stokesay once stood here: a pity it doesn't still. The rest of the village still straggles, apart from a slight tightening up at the turn of the road where there is a nice cottage range in two tone brickwork of the early 19th century, otherwise it is mostly modern infill, but not unattractive.

Summer 1996

TINGRITH

Of central Bedfordshire's estate villages Tingrith is among the most charming. Without being in any way spectacular in its architecture it nevertheless displays along the main street and the road leading to the church a delightful succession of Gothick villas and simple 18th-century cottages. The one fine though strangely asymmetrical Georgian façade of Tanqueray House seen in the drawing gives just the right urbane punctuation to the street. Its setting back from and at a higher level than the general building line give it added importance – perhaps rather more than it deserves.

The church is a gem and, considering its location in the middle of a district so much dedicated to Victorianization, almost a miracle in coming through the 19th century unscathed. By the south porch, in a position similar to that of the great ornate tomb at Chellington church, is a tomb in the Gothic taste of 1834, to Robert Trevor, esquire – a superb piece of craftsmanship even if a little like a wedding cake in style. It has suffered the loss of its ironwork, victim of the 'war effort': one trusts that the railings were not fated, like so much interesting ironwork, to rust slowly away on some scrap heap. The corner turrets of the chancel are very like those at Wymington in north Bedfordshire, though there is little likelihood of any connection between the two buildings.

Spring 1954

TODDINGTON

Some years ago I sketched this particular view for the *Bedfordshire Times*. I feel more than justified in doing it again, for Toddington is one of the most urbane of our villages, perhaps because it had the status of a market town in the past, with all the attendant wealth that that implied. By 1800 its importance was waning, the market house having been demolished the previous year, but the air of prosperity still lingers, and the grouping of the buildings around the central greens is one of the most satisfying in the County. The fine Georgian house in the illustration has been restored in recent years, and it is to the lasting credit of those responsible that the old village pond alongside has been converted so imaginatively into a little gem of free garden planning. There are no formal flower beds or railings, or the kind of suburban picturesque treatment that the *Architectural Review* so wittily calls 'God wottery'. The site is subtly contoured, the planting is informal, and the result is a complete delight. But is it not strange that a community which can create something so pleasing should tolerate such an abortion as the petrol sign in the middle of the green? The pumps and the garage itself, although utilitarian, are quite innocuous, but the sign sticks out like a sore thumb from all viewpoints. I have deliberately toned it down in the drawing. Surely the much vaunted Town and Country Planning Act could control this kind of thing? It can be harsh enough on the private builder and, rightly, on advertisements in towns; but out in the country it permits advertising and its attendant evils to riot unchecked.

St. George's Church, one of the best in the County, suffers from its Totternhoe stone construction and is in a constant state of decay, which intelligent restoration has tried to combat. Reinforcing with tiles in the tower, as at nearby Houghton Regis, has certainly given it a delightful quality of texture and colour.

Toddington lies 450 to 500 feet above sea level. One expects good views and they are in fact magnificent. The southern vistas towards the chalk hills are the most noted, and the best viewpoint is from the old earthworks of Congar Hill, but I prefer the north-west aspects. The range of the escarpment is certainly fine but mineral workings are biting into it at several points and hill-foot suburbanization is marring its character. North-westwards, however, there is fine rolling country to the Greensand ridge – a more intimate landscape altogether, bosky and with more than a memory of its densely wooded past.

Winter 1955

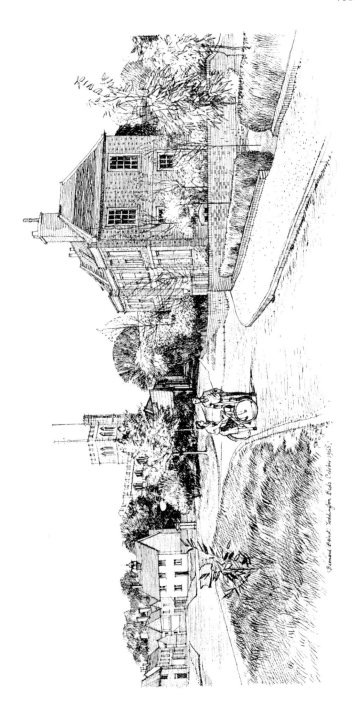

TOTTERNHOE KNOLLS

Westwards from Dunstable at the foot of the Five Knolls a long whale-back of lower downland stretches roughly north-westwards to terminate, after areas of scrub and fine beechwood, in Totternhoe Castle, a high knoll or beacon with rough grassy hillside dropping abruptly below it. This tongue of land, with its wide views of the great Chiltern scarp and rich vale of Aylesbury, and its slopes of scented, springy turf and thick woodland, forms an ideal playground for the neighbouring urban population. The more pathetic it is, therefore, to see the fearful inroads made by quarrying for chalk. Here one sees modern exploitation at work. With the suburban sprawl seeping over the hill from Dunstable it combines to reduce this once fair corner of the hills to a 'conquered country', as Massingham calls the Chilterns nearer London.

These Totternhoe Knolls are the site of stone quarries which throughout the Middle Ages supplied an area surprisingly extensive. My view is taken near the edge of the old workings, looking towards Leighton Buzzard. Earlier, the site had almost certainly been fortified and before that must have been a prehistoric lookout post over marshland below.

Wild life on the hills is varied and rich and the typical chalk flora in high summer is a delight. Many plants of considerable rarity have their home here, and insect, especially butterfly, population is in some ways almost unique.

It is devoutedly to be hoped that the action of the South Bedfordshire Preservation Society to defend the Knolls and the green ways will meet with the success it deserves, for if it were all to be quarried away the loss would be so great as to be unforgiveable.

Summer 1950

Bernard B West.

TURVEY
– The Chancel of the Church of All Saints

As a village Turvey starts and ends well from whichever way one approaches it. The possible and most unexpected exception is to be found after the uniquely attractive riverside road from Newton Blossomville, where the sewage disposal plant is sited and detailed in such a way as to do the maximum visual damage. Those responsible should be pilloried. The village itself has a grandeur which derives from extensive rebuilding in the 19th century, although here and there an original chimney stack or some Georgian fenestration points to the survival at the heart of many buildings of the older Turvey of Bradford Rudge's paintings and other topographical artists of the 1800s.

The church itself is the apotheosis of all that Victorian embellishment could achieve, where the village is grand, the church, or more particularly its chancel, is sumptuous. This is the Oxford Movement in all its archaeological and liturgical assurance. Internally one would never be deceived for a moment that this was a 14th-century chancel, the organ screen alone is a completely unmediaeval thing. Outside however one can see the sources, Dorchester Abbey for example or the curvilinear achievements of the Marshland such as Heckington, and it is all very plausible. Only close inspection of the label stops reveals the inevitable Victorian sentimentality of roses and lilies of the valley. Whether Scott's site supervision was close we shall probably never know, but his masons were master craftsmen and to be forgiven for the odd *jeu d'esprit* of elaboration.

The rest of the building is externally remarkably restrained in its restoration, with the exception of a particularly stupid and unjustifiable 'candle snuffer' on the tower, but inside, Gilbert Scott could probably not have been expected to tolerate the low Tudor arches at the end of the old nave, and these were swept away to be rebuilt in a form commensurate with the new chancel. Thus the interior today has a suspiciously smartened air but is nevertheless full of good things. Of these, apart from some delightful monuments, the one outstanding thing is a 13th-century crucifixion painting in the south aisle, which recently repaired and consolidated constitutes the most valuable church mural in the County.

Spring 1971

Turvey Church, the chancel
Richard B West. A.R.I.B.A.

UPPER DEAN

There are times when travelling round our much beleaguered County one is compelled to cry out in despair at the utter lack of feeling apparent in the many and varied ways which have been found to deface the landscape. Some of the worst are permanent or semi-permanent and only time and nature can effect a softening of harsh outlines and insensitive treatment of the land. One of the most insensitive agents in our lowland landscape, dependent as it is on the composition of groups of buildings and trees, is the Post Office with its proliferation of poles and wires. Our technology is still at a primitive stage with the telephone service, and it is the temporary, flimsy nature of the installations which reflects this; yet the harm the service does to the landscape is incalculable. Stripped of the clumsy tangle of wires and poles, this is the north Bedfordshire village at its most perfect. One knows for sure that siting of the distribution poles was planned only in two dimensions, and that nobody went to Dean to look at the church and assess the harm that would be done to views along the road. Is there never going to be a landscape consultant appointed to these statutory undertakings? Not now, presumably, as they can claim that there is no economic justification for such consideration – the mess can take the shortest routes and to hell with the view!

Dean is remote and very attractive in spite of silly infilling such as a daft piece of imitation Georgian on coming into the village, fancy dress of the most pretentious kind. There has been some really sensitive restoration and the Eileen Wade School is delightful both in scale and detail. It is All Saints' Church, however, which is very properly the crown, a building which survived derelict into a time when conservation was preferred to restoration. Thus it is that we have superb 15th-century roofs, carefully repaired, 16th-century pews, the old floors, and lovely though mutilated screens. One's only regret is the bareness of the walls, where plaster would make the interior perfect.

The landscape around the village with the removal of hedges is more open than formerly but saved by fine trees, and the apparent survival of more elms than is now the case further south. Yet another open winter so far will ensure the beetle/fungus combination another good season and one fears very much for such fine elms as those in the illustration.

Spring 1975

Upper Dean January 1975
Edmund Brett

UPPER GRAVENHURST

That one has only recently berated the telephone authority for its crimes
in the village scene at Upper Dean is no reason for not having another bash
at more crass insensitivity at Upper Gravenhurst. This is another of those
perfect relationships of church and village which are easy enough to draw but
impossible to photograph. This view is hopelessly mutilated with poles and
wires in all directions and anyone interested in seeing just how much harm
this can do to our surroundings might care to take the magazine and stand
on the viewpoint for the drawing. What we take for granted everywhere, our
ubiquitous street furniture is to the greater glory of the engineer, at his most
insensitive. Our towns and villages are full of poles, barriers, bins and clutter
and we take this dreadful tide of bits and pieces entirely for granted as it
threatens to engulf us. No one is likely to see Gravenhurst as worth the cost
of freeing from poles and wire, even in the centre, and yet it is an attractive
little place. Of course nowhere, near to both Luton and Bedford, has escaped
the infilling of the last twenty years and the hard and regular outlines of
modern housing now dominate the softer lines of the old settlement.

The church is surrounded on west and north sides by a 'close' of houses
facing into the churchyard; only one has the proper colour and texture as
a foil to the church; too many of the others are roofed in a variety of hard
and insensitive materials, such as painted corrugated iron, for them to
be acceptable as truly of village character. Most of the church, however,
is attractively textured in very dark sandstone with some brick infill and
dressings. The chancel strikes the only discordant note, a harsh Victorian
rebuilding in which the tracery of the fenestration is nothing if not wilful,
and certainly not based on any likely earlier design.

Summer 1976

Upper Gravenhurst.
April 9th 1976. Dennis B. West.

UPPER STONDON – Church of All Saints

The fact that a 13th-century doorway survives from an original church allows speculation on the 1857 rebuilding of All Saints. Such an eccentric little building might be some sort of memory of an earlier structure. Why for instance the higher chancel and an east window which, were it genuine, would indicate that magical changeover in the 1350s when the very English late gothic style emerged? Probably no more than scholarship and competence, but one wonders. The porch tower has a precedent at Langford but here is almost domestic. Another intriguing thing is the masonry itself, all sandstone, some of the blocks more massive than would have been employed in the Victorian period. One cannot escape the conclusion that this is re-used material, particularly as there are signs of weathering which could pre-date the 1850s.

The settlement of this plateau must have been early, perhaps pre-Conquest. The 12th-century St. Thomas' Chapel at Chapel Farm in neighbouring Meppershall is just over the hill. Clearance and drainage here should have been easier than in the valley between Stondon and Shillington, another hilltop settlement of early foundation and now an element in the wonderful view to the south, where our portion of the Chilterns assumes a magnificence quite comparable with the much vaunted scarp to the south-west in Buckinghamshire.

It is a pity that the water tower is such a brute; when are we going to produce the lovely free sculptured towers which form such an attractive element in the French countryside? They make a feature of them over there but we still seem to be stuck with the solidity of the 1930s. Still, I suppose it is a landmark, even if a somewhat brooding one.

Spring 1992

WARDEN ABBEY

Next to Sutton packhorse bridge this building has been recorded as much as any piece of architecture in Bedfordshire. My reasons for illustrating it again are twofold: first, it is in such an appalling structural condition that I doubt whether it will survive for many more years; and secondly the site is in the news after the recent first trial excavation by the Bedford Archaeological Society.

The Abbey itself has completely disappeared except for one large buttress contained in the existing structure. This single mediaeval feature was used as a guide in the excavations. The red-brick mansion is post-Suppression of the mid-16th century and survived until 1790 when it was reduced to the present pathetic fragment. The well known drawing by the brothers Buck is of the north elevation but it is practically impossible to reconcile it with any part of the present north side. Whether they were inaccurate, or whether the little that is left has been tampered with, is now impossible to tell. Excavation certainly exposed the line of the walls extending to the west, together with quantities of attained glass that may have been knocked out of the big oriel window shown in the Buck engraving but it will need further digging to sort out 16th- and 17th-century footings from the mediaeval work.

As a whole the excavation was tantalizing, and it is still too early to attempt interpretation of the walls uncovered. A wall line ran from the buttress as expected, but whether of the chancel or the south face of a transept is uncertain. The general building materials seemed to be a course of large pebbles rammed into a trench carrying large slabs of local sandstone; these in turn carried the masonry of the main walls. There had apparently been a lot of internal Totternhoe stonework, and one 'robber trench' was full of carved fragments of this material. When one remembers that four hundred cartloads of stone were taken to Bedford for building work in the 18th century it is not surprising that so little survives. The much publicised skeleton found near some enormous sandstone footings was something of an embarrassment. In its position it was quite unexpected and had every appearance of being pre-Christian, but was certainly not of the Bronze Age as was reported in several newspapers.

Autumn 1960

Old Warden Abbey. August 19
Bernard West.

WESTONING
– Church of St. Mary Magdalene

The Flitwick-Westoning urbanisation happened in pre-planning days, and if ever there is a visible justification for subsequent legislation, these two parishes provide the evidence. One is thankful that the McIntyre Trust is building something so attractive at Church End; the cause is a very worthy one and the realisation of it in a sort of refined log cabin idiom with asbestos cement slates produces a happy holiday camp effect which is as far removed from the institutional as can be. Otherwise infilling and sprawl have been on a fairly intense scale. The work of the 19th and early 20th centuries was to blot out the relationship of village to country, and infilling later was obviously difficult to resist. There are delightful surprises: one modern house in black feather-edged boarding and white trim, glimpsed at the end of the lane is self-confident if a little 'House and Garden'. Before it, much enlarged and altered, is a fine 17th-century timber-framed house, and opposite the old Parsonage with its magnificent trees provides a fine setting for the church.

St. Mary Magdalene is mostly early 14th century with much renewed geometrical tracery in some windows. One can believe most of the restoration but it is a little heartless. Inside, delicate arcades and chancel arch point to the early 1300s. The spire reminds one of that at Wootton, later work of the 1450s, but the rebuilding of the parapet in Victorian times could have been more in sympathy with the sandstone wall below.

Summer 1975

Church End Westoning
Dennis F. West. 1975. April

WILDEN

The South Brook enforces a happy linear character on Wilden. From Church End Farm to Lower East End Farm settlement is scattered along the stream side, often on the south bank, which a variety of little bridges link to the main road on the north, a simple geographical fact that produces a complex and always interesting relationship between one side of the water and the other. The views from the churchyard to the *Victoria Arms* or to Manor Farm rely as much on the enforced separation of boundaries and their treatment as on the richness of the tree cover with which the village is so well endowed.

The school, the 'pub' and the group of cottages in my drawing are three sides of a little grass square, disposed in a way that could hardly be bettered. Perhaps the bridge would be improved if its undoubtedly second-hand municipal railings were replaced by simple horizontal slats.

Dignified but without great architectural character, the church is a simple 15th-century aisleless building; but the belfry openings are of a sophisticated design elongated to a happy proportion in relation to the belfry stage of the tower. Inside, the chancel roof is an admirable piece of 15th-century carpentry, marred now because the angel corbels have been painted a soapy pale blue by some misguided hand and, insult added to injury, in an objectionable glossy finish. St. Nicolas suffers from the all too common indignity of a blocked tower arch, redeemed only by a magnificent blazon of the Royal Arms, which could do with a thorough clean and a coat of varnish. The monument of 1643 to Jasper Fisher is a competent piece of shop-work in Chelleston alabaster. That to Richard Cradocke Chalke, who lost his life at the hands of the Japanese in 1942, is a reminder of events that, for all their recent horror, have now passed into the long pageant of history which this remote country church has witnessed.

Winter 1961

Wilden. November 1961
Bernard B Wood.

WILLINGTON – Stables

A fine architectural group of church, stables and dovecote is all that remains of manorial Willington of Sir John Gostwick, master of the horse to Cardinal Wolsey. The dovecote with its double pitched roof and 'crow-stepped' gables is outside the range of my picture to the left. Its neighbour the stable block of about 1520 is in the same style with bold and simple details. It is of two storeys, with moulded ceiling beams inside. The stepping of the gables is generally considered to be of Flemish derivation; and certainly as one goes into Cambridgeshire and East Anglia, the country of the Flemish weavers' adoption, such attractive roof treatment becomes increasingly common.

But even so charming and rare a scene has not escaped unscathed. Gravel-digging presents an appalling foreground to the church as seen from the Bedford road. We are apt to think that the horrors of open-cast digging are a distant phenomenon, but here is a waste land in our own territory. Time and nature will be the only salvation of the scene.

Spring 1952

Willington. February 1952 Bernard B West

WILLINGTON – Church of St. Lawrence

One makes no excuse for returning to the incomparable group at Willington of church, dovecote, stables and manor. Rarity value seems to dictate the fame and frequent representation of dovecote and stables, quite apart from the status of National Trust ownership. Somehow the church, St. Lawrence, doesn't rate the same attention, but it is very much of a piece with the old Manor outbuildings. Some ambiguity attaches to Sir John Gostwick's epitaph of 1541 (though he died in 1545); it refers to 'this work' which could apply to the north chapel but more probably refers to the whole church. One often wonders whether people like the Gostwicks, near to the court and for obvious reasons only too well aware of the uncertain temper of the biggest thug there has ever been on the English throne, had any idea of the gathering storm. The dissolution of Newnham, from which the building materials for Willington undoubtedly came, was only a prelude to the social changes of 1543–46 when war speeded up the sale of monastic and church lands. Newnham was dissolved in 1540 and by then Henry VIII was totally isolated from Europe, and Catholic invasion a possibility. This was the time when our most refined late Gothic building was carefully completed, though the fan vault planned for the chancel was never carried out, a fitting crown to the building which we shall never see.

Historians will remember in January 1540 Henry married the 'Flanders Mare', the marriage lasted six months and Cromwell was executed just after the divorce. One would love to know where John Gostwick as Treasurer of the First Fruits to Henry stood in all this – probably, as we would say today, with a very low profile.

The stained glass has gone and the rood screen. It is, however, still a magnificent building and later Gostwicks join John in the north chapel. Strange to think that Edward almost lived on to the time of William Laud, dying in 1630; his wife in 1633, when Laud was made Archbishop of Canterbury.

Henry Clutton had a go at the church in 1879 but mercifully not radically. It is interesting to note that in the chancel he copied tiles from Warden

Abbey, to repair the chancel paving – a design of two Talbots rampant, which turned up again in the 1960s excavations at the Abbey and which were possibly brought to the church in the first instance by Bradford Rudge, art master at Bedford Modern School in the 1850s. He excavated at Old Warden, trench following and rather brutally, but at least he was largely responsible for persuading the Duke of Bedford, then owner of the estate, not to demolish the stables and dovecote. Some of the original tiles are also used in the chancel and obviously the mould for the copies was derived from these.

Spring 1986

WILSTEAD

Before the last World War one remembers the meadows of Wilstead, particularly to the south of the village, hummocky, full of cowslips, green winged orchids and mushrooms, with high blackberry hedges and old trees. This was before the advent of the Royal Ordnance Depot; and though in bemoaning a lost Arcadia one is remembering a landscape of agricultural depression, its total destruction was unforgivable. Like so much wartime 'land grab' the mess has become permanent with mutations through refugee camp, dereliction and discount warehousing.

Small wonder the village reflects this urbanisation, and being on the A6 has also suffered the effects which are inevitably associated with a main road. The estates have followed: Types A, B and C straight from the developers' appropriate drawer, 'three-bed semi', 'three-bed detached', 'four-bed detached' etc., dapple light facings, Redland tiles, standard standardisation. As an architect one's heart sinks at what rising land values and population mobility have brought about, and how we as a profession have become the manipulators of the clip-on-cliché. Amidst all this anonymity is the heart of the old village, as much as anything a parking lot for the activity of the crossroads.

All Saints, almost dwarfed by its gargantuan, rambling and now derelict rectory, is hemmed in on the south by the pale north walls of the estate, but the churchyard is well timbered and preserves its unity. The church in all its external details is essentially Victorian, although it is reasonable to assume they follow original forms. More could be made of this little cul-de-sac; a case for judicious infilling which so often can in fact mean the loss of just those gaps and breathing spaces which actually articulate some villages. One little 19th-century villa has been entirely faced in artificial stone, the frightening result of which has been to create a complete alien. It might just be lost sight of in the Peak District, here it is a joke, and not a very good one.

So what about such a village, or Wootton or Houghton Conquest nearby? Here the salvation might actually be urbanisation as a ring of small satellite towns to Bedford, compact, high rise and intimate (some buildings appropriate to such a change of identity have already been built). If it means saving other sites and countryside it might be worthwhile.

Spring 1973

WOBURN – High Street

Here the tourist reigns, but for some reason only as far as the crossroads; to penetrate to the southern section of the High Street, and incidentally be rewarded by both the most beautiful pub in the County and a 'Georgian' filling station, is for many to cross the great divide. The visitors' Woburn is here in the gentrified milieu of antiques, boutiques and general catering, from the country house ambience of the hotel to its folksy variants at public house level. Few seem to walk far along the street to the north or west, and not many on evidence discover Clutton's incredible St. Mary's church, a scholarly elephantine essay in *Ile de France* Romanesque.

It is a good thing then that central Woburn is so magnificent, and that so many original shop fronts have survived to this time when there is a justification for their retention. One recognises so well in Chipping Camden, Burford, Stratford-upon-Avon, the same phenomenon, the dress shop awash with genteel tweeds in tasteful autumn tints, the various levels of antique shop from bric-a-brac (gonks, large sub-Beardsley prints, etc.), to the sort of over-priced museum at the upper level. Saddlery and general tack features somewhere, a high quality bookshop, and inevitable pottery. All the same such emporia preserve the fabric of the place, and one is thankful at Woburn that real small town shops, the grocer in the centre for instance, share the scene with their more specialised neighbours.

It is above the level of cars and advertising that real architecture rewards are to be found, particularly the work of the mid-1740s on the east side of the High Street. Here the segmented arched windows are richly modelled with rubbed brick arches, carved keystones, carved brick aprons below the cills and red brickwork combined with dark glazed to pattern the walls themselves. On top of all this richness are giant angle and, in one case, central pilasters carried through two floors and finished in Roman Doric capitals in carved brickwork. Such work compares readily with more famous examples of post-fire Georgian rebuilding, such as that by the Bastard brothers at Blandford. Only to the south of the lovely spiky town hall, a sort of Jacobean gothic folly, is there a nasty gap.

Here, doubtless as a sacrifice to traffic requirements, we have lost the essential tightening-up in the grain of the town. Opposite to the *Bedford Arms* there was and should be a strong foursquare Georgian block for the loss of which John Gedge's tasteful neo-Georgian beyond is not quite sufficient compensation. But this is the only defect in an otherwise perfect town, and a minor one, for beyond, in that southern no man's land, is the perfect townscape element, a building looking down the street to turn a corner, making a pivot before the more rural and just as attractive southern part of the town begins.

Winter 1977

WOBURN – Chapel

The contrast between the hearty French Gothic of Clutton's new church on the edge of the park and the present chapel designed by Blore in 1868, on the site of the old St. Mary's, could not be greater. Clutton never seemed able or inclined to extend the vocabulary of English Gothic, preferring a wild and sinewy Jacobean or vigorous echoes of Anjou. Blore however could stretch and interpret late Gothic to some effect. One should not judge him by the mutilated Pitt Press in Cambridge or even the sad facades of Bedford's Harpur Centre, a thin veil to the commercial mayhem behind. The latter was once much more picturesque with pinnacled niches on the gables, long since swept away. Here he has used the base of the old mediaeval tower to raise what Pevsner accurately describes as 'a very pretty piece of confectionery'. There are all sorts of echoes: St. Peter's, Irthlingborough or St. Peter's at Lowick, for example, not all that far away in Northamptonshire. One can see the benefits of such unashamed eclecticism when the details are synthesised as cleverly as here. The ogee curve to the buttress gables and the main pinnacles is a delightful detail which gives great animation to the silhouette. The chapel in contrast is somewhat squat, but generally sound though totally unmediaeval.

The old school next door is certainly late Tudor and from a distance could be a Nene Valley building, only here the ferruginous stone is from our own Greensand. Blore was quite restrained in his conversion and restoration; only the double chimney stack is an obvious insertion with strangely clumsy mismatching of the masonry courses. Windows in the east gable show the mistake of using Totternhoe stone for fine architectural detail. Blore's porch to the street is great fun and with the wall to the churchyard completes a most picturesque and irregular group amid the Georgian splendours that surround it. The 1850 almshouses to the north break the classical theme as well but are not 'centre stage' as it were.

We are really lucky with Woburn, as great an experience as the Bastards' Blandford in far away Dorset; perhaps even better, being under less pressure; but sitting drawing one realises just how horrendous is the ceaseless grind of traffic.

Summer 1992

Woburn May 17ᵗʰ 92
Bernard Fisk, R.I.B.A.

WOOTTON

Poor besieged Wootton, dumping ground of the overspill that Kempston could not quite absorb, the monument, one might almost say the textbook example, of all the errors into which planning control can fall. Not urban, not rural, not even quite suburban, but an appalling grafting of estates of various designs on to what was in any case a fairly amorphous village. What a monument to the 1960s and 1970s; perhaps as we suggested in 1973 at Wilstead one might as well really urbanise these Bedford satellite villages as they have been so grossly betrayed. Not that erecting blocks of flats alongside thatched cottages is the way to do it. The crass insensitivity that allowed this to happen, obviously without any site study, is perhaps less common today. We are in the era of design guides and conservation areas, but the unqualified designer, and indeed the rogue architect, should study Wootton. '*Si monumentum requiris circumspice*'.

Here and there the old Bedfordshire of the compact community can still be evoked. Hemmed in by estates, all hi-fi and Cortinas, is the church and its neighbours even here in some fancy dress more appropriate to the Dordogne than the English Midlands; then turn round and, although the skeleton of the old relationship of land and settlement survives, brick chimneys close the view. It is all the more tantalising because both worlds confront each other. There is, of course, nothing wrong with the consumer society, it is our bed and we perforce lie on it, but with such poignant contrasts our loyalties are questioned. Little of the old way of life of church and manor can be defended in contemporary terms but is the replacement so preferable?

The fabric of this survival at Wootton is the House, late 17th century, quite simple, somewhat falsified by recent modifications; the church and the perfectly sited cottages of my illustration. After one more group of cottages the world of the estates begins. The church is mainly 14th century in date, quite early but heavily restored in 1860, a bad time, but things could have been worse. The best things in the church are undoubtedly the chancel tablets to Humphrey and Philip Monoux, 1685 and 1707, the later one by Edward Stanton.

Winter 1976

Wootton October. 1976.
Dennis B West

WRESTLINGWORTH

To the east of Potton a long hill brings one to the plateau where a shelter belt forms a sort of frontier to the open empty prospect beyond. An unbroken view from Baldock to the outskirts of Cambridge, it is of course the post-enclosure landscape of the combine age; the same view as that from Cockayne Hatley churchyard. The elms have gone, the hedges and even the wayside trees. Before the village, there survive two fine whitebeams, one of the rare ones with leaves halfway between mountain ash and *sorbus aria*, relict of some village improvement like the lovely wayside planting to the east of Pavenham, but nothing else. To someone's lasting credit there is new tree planting at one point, oaks with conifers to pull them up, which will be of the highest landscape value in fifty years' time.

So one comes to Wrestlingworth where the village trees assume more importance in the landscape than most of the buildings, which are generally mediocre. In essence the older pattern has gone; the *Chequers* and one or two cottages have the Cambridgeshire flavour which is familiar beyond Orwell to the east but much is modern though well absorbed by planting. Around the church things improve, but don't hang together; one would love to be able to relate the dumpy church tower to Ivy Cottage in the north-west corner but it can't be done. Nor can the cottage on the hill or the school, individually excellent, be combined in a satisfactory view.

The school, a product of the enlightened Stan Goodman era at the County Architect's Department, is right in scale and texture and recent fencing is equally appropriate. So one is content to come upon the various buildings in their own context, with only Ivy Cottage on the corner, of 1829, not quite *ornee* but highly picturesque, making for the effect of a small close. A modern house to the east takes up the rhythm of the fenestration of this cottage on a grand scale, and to great effect.

The church, locked as usual, in this case 'on police advice', is small in scale and brutally restored, but the interior is still thankfully a village church and the churchyard unprettified. There is a lovely knobbly bunch of tombstones on the south side which look like a bulk order at the end of the 17th century from Ketton or one of the mass production quarries; one wonders if this is the legacy of a particular epidemic. One hopes for resistance to any proposals for tidying up this particular patch as has been done, probably for easy mowing, to the west and north.

Winter 1983

Wrestlingworth, Ivy Cottage from the Churchyard
Bannister Sept. 1983

WREST PARK – The Archer Pavilion

The main survivor of the buildings on Rocque's print of 1735 is this delightfully gawky piece of English baroque by Thomas Archer (1668–1743), companion in style to his demolished Hill House. It seems that many of the well known designers of the 18th century worked for the Duke of Kent: the Bowling Green House, for example, was designed by Batty Langley (1696–1751), notorious for his preposterous attempt to systemize Gothic architecture into a parallel of the Classical orders. The Pavilion is typical of Archer, most wayward of English baroque architects, more so in many ways than Vanbrugh, but compared with the Baroque of southern Catholic Europe he created a style of composition out of inharmonious elements that has more in common with Italian Mannerism of the late 17th century.

Wrest was rebuilt for Earl de Grey in 1834 in a passable Louis XVI idiom; the very English formalism of the old elevation is now to be seen only in Rocque's illustrations and the early formalism of the grounds shown on his plans was later replaced by the romantic landscape of 'Capability' Brown (1716–1783). In the main the grounds retain their former garden architecture, of which the Pavilion at the end of its long canal is the most satisfying. After the French pavilions and the mistletoe in the tall poplars framing a distant view of hills that could easily border the Seine, Archer's work seems strangely English and provincial, which is anything but the case when considered in the context of the early 18th century.

Commendation must be made for the excellent care given to the estate by the Institute of Agricultural Engineering. That Lancelot Brown's landscape should have matured when the great days of the house are over is an irony of history which matters little now that it has been inherited by such responsible trustees.

Summer 1964

Bernard B West.
Wrest Park April 1984.

WYMINGTON

It is characteristic of the 'boot and shoe' town of the upper Nene Valley that in juxtaposition there are often dignified village centres, around a magnificent church, with a mean industrial sprawl beyond. This consists mostly of rows of bleak streets which have taken away the identity of the place; both the original town or village and its landscape setting. This has been the major crime, the meanness and wastage of land, the actual industry, iron mining and smelting, and the shoe factories are at least something with a strong identity and are almost preferable.

Wymington is the one Bedfordshire village which belongs to this minor black country; Rushden has drained its character away and what should have been a compact valley village is now largely amorphous and bleak. Experiments in the use of essentially urban forms for new housing have been a disaster both in siting and materials, an excuse for which misguided planning policies must take a large share of the blame. It is only around the church and Manor Farm where the village could be saved. Oliver Carey's additions to the Church of England school are a delight, and of course at St. Lawrence we have our one Nene Valley church, not perhaps on a scale to compare with the amazing buildings at Raunds and Higham Ferrars but rich in quality and detail. Whatever designers John Curteys used, they were conservative in style for a known start to the building in 1350, using a rich late Curvilinear which by then was old fashioned.

Manor Farm and its associated buildings, though now all empty and disused, make a wonderful composition stepping down the slope to the west. Any development should preserve this sort of character as well as the invaluable cordon sanitaire between this end of the village and the dreary suburbia to the north.

At the time this drawing was done one of the most gorgeous Romany caravans to be seen in our area had taken winter quarters on the site. On sale now as its owners are getting to the stage where a modern caravan, with all its comforts, is needed for their old age, it stands for the nomadic life, yet is more indigenous than the sprawl of villas beyond. The suburban society which has made a waste of Wymington could look at the care and craftsmanship of that caravan to some profit. It is a real irony that in their new accommodation these true Romanies will soon become as anonymous as the tinkers they despise, and their traditions lost as completely as those one has mourned in this slightly bilious article.

Winter 1972

YELDEN

In many ways this is a primitive little place, apparently out of the sphere of prosperity which has come to so much of North Bedfordshire; Riseley had this 'back of beyond' quality not so long ago and to some extent Dean and Shelton have it still. The village tends to be made up of uncomfortable contrasts, the outlying buildings of the aerodrome, thin in detail, cheap and incongruous, dominate as one comes down the hill from Melchbourne, and shatter the unity of church and village, and yet in the foreground the castle site rises in finely sculptured earthworks quite unblemished. There is much fine individual building, some in stone, deep thatch and nice groupings, but a lot of decay, corrugated iron, and that special sort of backyard litter which is peculiar to the less well-to-do village, ashes, old sticks, strange little huts and sheds covered with lino and vans parked in cottage gardens. But the village is still there and much of it could be very fine. Strung out along the narrow valley of the Till, it is perhaps one of the places where some sensitive infilling would revitalise the rest, as it has undoubtedly done in other parts of north Bedfordshire.

The church, finely sited on a spur above the village, has a steeple more characteristic of distant Rutland than the adjoining Nene Valley; one can think of several around the Vale of Catmose such as Hambleton to which this could be the twin. It is characteristic of them that the towers tend to be disproportionately tall to the dumpy spires.

To the south and west of the village the remains of the open field system confirm that the village has never been officially enclosed. It is likely, therefore, that Top, Middle and Manor Farms acquired land gradually from the end of the 19th century and that therein may lie the clue to the waning of community life.

Spring 1966

Yelden January 1966.
Bernard E West.

BRIDGES OF TIME

Shela Porter

The unfolding of a traumatic span of seventy years, this gripping autobiography tells the story of a woman's struggle, mostly in Bedford, to achieve happiness as she battles against fate and finally finds contentment in her later years.

The third in a large family of eight children, Shela enjoys early years at school and writes small stories each week for her teacher on pieces of toilet paper. Marriage at twenty and the birth of three children in the first three years lead to a lonely life on a council estate as her marriage breaks down and her violent and immature husband leaves the family home. The oldest boy leaves home to live with his father and Shela meets her second husband who promises to look after them all. Now widowed and lonely as her other children leave home, Shela begins a questionable relationship with a man whom she eventually marries after his strictly Catholic wife dies. Her unhappiness with an unfaithful and controlling husband results in a nervous breakdown and a return to Bedford with a pressing need to re-establish her life yet again.

In her early sixties, with all thoughts of romance firmly dismissed from her mind, she meets the caring and gentle man who becomes her new husband and who nurses her back to health while encouraging her to write regularly again.

THREADS OF TIME

Shela Porter

A pale-faced city child is evacuated from London during the Zeppelin raids of 1917. In Hitchin she takes a dressmaking apprenticeship and opens her own workshop with customers including the local gentry and the young Flora Robson.

Moving to Bedford on her marriage, her sewing skills help her rapidly growing family to survive the Depression; working long hours during the exigencies of war-time Britain, it is her re-designed battle-jacket that Glenn Miller is wearing when he disappears over the Channel in 1944, and entertainers Bing Crosby and Bob Hope leave comics and candy for her 'cute kids'. For five years after the war the family run a small café in the town but sewing then sees her through again as the business is sold, she is widowed with a nine-year-old son to raise, all her children gradually leave and she moves away to be wardrobe mistress to a big operatic society in High Wycombe. Finally she settles in a small cottage opposite the great airship sheds at Cardington from where she once watched the ill-fated R101 take off on its last journey in 1930.

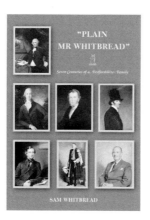

"PLAIN MR WHITBREAD"
Seven Centuries of a Bedfordshire Family

Sam Whitbread

The Whitbread family have been a part of Bedfordshire life since at least the 13th Century (and probably earlier). From small beginnings as peasant farmers, through appointments as local officials to the founder of the Brewery, one of the most notable success stories of the Industrial Revolution, and his son, the radical Whig politician and follower of Fox, the Whitbreads have gradually made their presence felt, first locally and later nationally. Six Whitbreads sat in the House of Commons for a total of 128 years, while at the same time building roads, bridges and hospitals, improving cottages and the local churches, and serving as magistrates, High Sheriffs and Lord-Lieutenants of the County.

The book's title is taken from the fact that at least two members of the family were offered peerages but preferred to "remain plain Mr Whitbread".

The author originally conceived the book as a simplified family history for his children and grandchildren but it will also appeal to all those interested in the local history of Bedfordshire.

The narrative ends with the death of the author's father in 1985, but the author has added a "postscript" outlining the first seventy years of his own life.

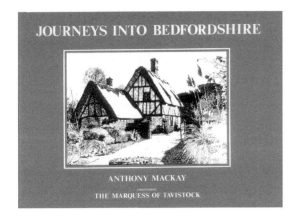

JOURNEYS INTO BEDFORDSHIRE

Anthony Mackay

This book of ink drawings reveals an intriguing historic heritage and captures the spirit of England's rural heartland, ranging widely over cottages and stately homes, over bridges, churches and mills, over sandy woods, chalk downs and watery river valleys.

Every corner of Bedfordshire has been explored in the search for material, and, although the choice of subjects is essentially a personal one, the resulting collection represents a unique record of the environment today.

The notes and maps, which accompany the drawings, lend depth to the books, and will assist others on their own journeys around the counties.

Anthony Mackay's pen-and-ink drawings are of outstanding quality. An architectural graduate, he is equally at home depicting landscapes and buildings. The medium he uses is better able to show both depth and detail than any photograph.

EXPLORING HISTORY ALL AROUND

Vivienne Evans

A handbook of local history, arranged as a series of routes to cover Bedfordshire and adjoining parts of Hertfordshire and Buckinghamshire. It is organised as two books in one. There are seven thematic sections full of fascinating historical detail and anecdotes for armchair reading. Also it is a perfect source of family days out as the book is organised as circular motoring/cycling explorations, highlighting attractions and landmarks. Also included is a background history to all the major towns in the area, plus dozens of villages, which will enhance your appreciation and understanding of the history that is all around you!

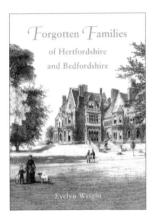

FORGOTTEN FAMILIES
of Hertfordshire and Bedfordshire

Evelyn Wright

This book tells the story of families once famous but whose fame is now mainly forgotten. They all lived in Hertfordshire and Bedfordshire in the 16th and 17th centuries, and include the Bechers of Renhold (of Becher's Brook fame), the Mordaunts of Turvey Abbey, Lady Cathcart of Tewin, the Bull family of Hertford, the Nodes family of Stevenage, the Docuras of Lilley and the Wicked Lady of Markyate Cell. All the families were related to each other, forming an intricate network over two counties: Hertfordshire and Bedfordshire. The author is one of their 20th century descendants. The book includes pedigrees showing the relationship between various families, and illustrations of many of the manor houses and mansions in which they lived.

Evelyn Wright was born in the village of Wingfield in Suffolk, and moved to Bedfordshire soon after her marriage in 1952. During a busy life bringing up five children, running a Nursery School and looking after elderly parents, she has always found time for writing. Evelyn is married to John Wright, a Chartered Surveyor, and they live in Aspley Heath in Bedfordshire.

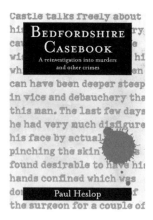

Castle talks freely about
hi**BEDFORDSHIRE**ry
ca**CASEBOOK**e
wi A reinvestigation into murders hi
wh and other crimes en
can have been deeper steep
in vice and debauchery the
this man. The last few days
he had very much disfigure
his face by actual
pinching the skin
found desirable to have his
hands confined which was
do Paul Heslop f
the surgeon for a couple of

BEDFORDSHIRE CASEBOOK
A reinvestigation into murders and other crimes

Paul Heslop

This is a book about crime and punishment in Bedfordshire. It focuses mainly on the time when perpetrators were hanged for murder and lesser crimes, or sentenced to hard labour, or transported abroad for what today would be regarded as minor offences.

They range from the 17th century incarceration of John Bunyan, whose 'crime' was to preach outwith the established church; to rape and terror perpetrated by the man they called The Fox, on the South Bedfordshire borders in the 1980s. 'Domestic violence' features: the brutal murder of his wife by Joseph Castle in Luton in 1859, and the murder of 23-year-old Ruby Annie Keen at Leighton Buzzard by Leslie George Stone in 1937. We have the murder of Old Sally Marshall, at Little Staughton, in 1870; a Luton mugging that ended up as murder when William Worsley, convicted on the evidence of an accomplice, was hanged; and the A6 murder at Deadman's Hill, the infamous Hanratty case, still topical today.

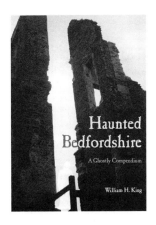

HAUNTED BEDFORDSHIRE
A Ghostly Compendium

William H.King

This book describes over one hundred and forty well known haunted sites throughout Bedfordshire. It also gives ideas on how to investigate such haunted locations including details of useful equipment, along with sections on orbs, ghostly noises and materialisations.

Ampthill a spectral knight in armour plus haunted ruins.

Bedford a haunted shopping arcade and a gruesome ghost.

Dunstable phantom monks, a flirtatious spirit and a buried witch.

Houghton Regis the ghosts of a Saxon Chieftain and a young girl.

Kensworth the spirits of a headless milkmaid and an angry witch.

Leighton Buzzard haunted pubs and a very violent poltergeist.

Luton cinema and museum ghosts plus a phantom dog.

Millbrook an incorporeal horse with a headless rider.

Riseley a haunted farm and the spectre of a nurse.

Sandy a headless woman walking her pet dog.

Toddington ghosts in nearly every pub.

Wilden a haunted ruin? You decide.

Woburn haunted Woburn Abbey.

FROM SAXONS TO SPEED
A New History of Old Bedford

Ian Freeman

The early history of Bedford town has been treated in a somewhat perfunctory way by previous local historians. This is understandable because information from the "Dark Ages" is sparse whereas there is a plethora of information readily available from later centuries.

This book is an attempt to fill that gap, using what firm information there is, supplemented by intelligent speculation when necessary. As a result, a number of generally accepted "facts" are put into question, and, in some cases, shown to be wrong.

The book begins with the Saxon period through the times of King Offa and King Alfred when the settlement and basic structure of the town was being laid out. It goes on to the Norman and Platagenet periods and describes how those invaders and rulers left their mark on the town.

Finally, it looks at the town as depicted in John Speed's map of the town which he published in 1610. It describes those streets and buildings which have survived from that time and discusses some of the prominent people who have lived in the town from time to time.